Physics P1

Introduction

Welcome to your *Activate* 1 Workbook. This Workbook contains lots of practice questions and activities to help you to progress through the course.

Each chapter from the *Activate* 1 Student Book is covered and includes a summary of all the content you need to know. Answers to all of the questions are in the back of the Workbook so you will be able to see how well you have answered them.

Practice activities – Lots of questions and activities, increasing in difficulty, give you plenty of practice and help to build your confidence.

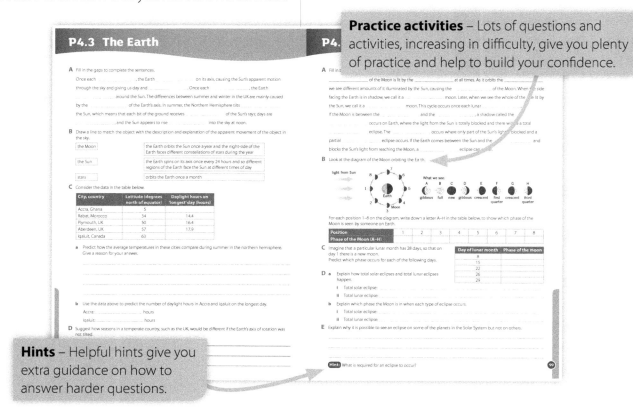

Hints – Helpful hints give you extra guidance on how to answer harder questions.

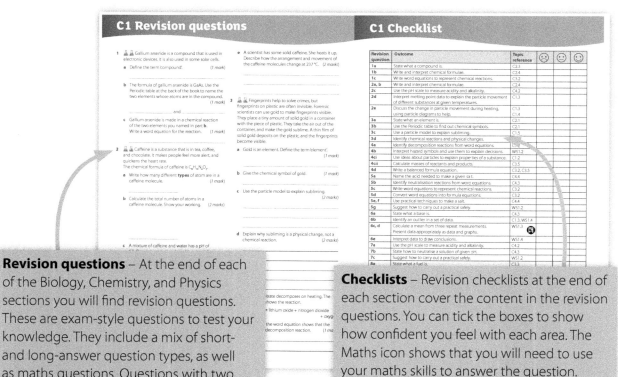

Revision questions – At the end of each of the Biology, Chemistry, and Physics sections you will find revision questions. These are exam-style questions to test your knowledge. They include a mix of short- and long-answer question types, as well as maths questions. Questions with two conical flasks next to them are the easiest; questions with three flasks are harder.

Checklists – Revision checklists at the end of each section cover the content in the revision questions. You can tick the boxes to show how confident you feel with each area. The Maths icon shows that you will need to use your maths skills to answer the question.

Oxford KS3 Science

Activate
Question • Progress • Succeed

1

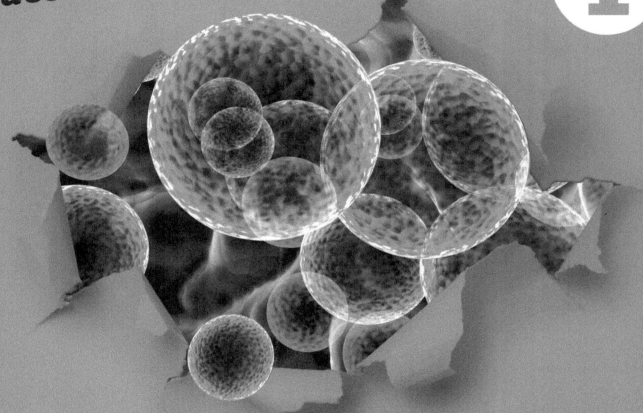

Workbook: Higher
Including Diagnostic Pinchpoint activities

Jon Clarke
Philippa Gardom Hulme
Jo Locke

Assessment Editor
Dr Andrew Chandler-Grevatt

OXFORD
UNIVERSITY PRESS

Contents

Pinchpoints

A Pinchpoint is an idea or concept in science that can be challenging to learn. It is often difficult to say *why* these ideas are challenging to learn. The Pinchpoint intervention question at the end of each chapter focuses on a challenging idea from within the chapter. By answering the Pinchpoint question you will see whether you understand the concept or whether you have gone wrong. By doing the follow-up activity you will find out why you made the mistake and how to correct it.

Pinchpoint question – The Pinchpoint question is about a difficult concept from the chapter that students often get wrong. You should answer the Pinchpoint question and one follow-up activity. The Pinchpoint is multiple choice; answer the question by choosing a letter and then do the follow-up activity with the same letter.

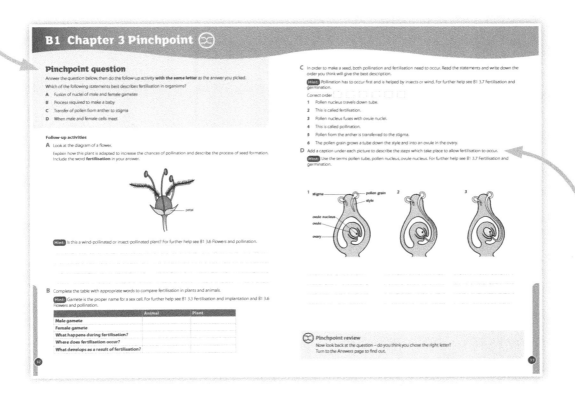

Pinchpoint follow-up – The follow-up activities will help you to better understand the difficult concept. If you got the Pinchpoint question right, the follow-up will develop your understanding further. If you got the Pinchpoint wrong, it will help you to see why you went wrong, and how to get it right next time.

WS1.1 Asking scientific questions
WS1.2 Planning investigations

A Fill in the gaps to complete the sentences.

The plan for an investigation starts with the scientific _____ you are trying to answer. You should make a _____ about what the answer might be, and use your scientific _____ to explain your prediction.

In your plan you should identify the _____ variable you will change, the _____ variable you will measure or observe, and a list of variables you will _____. Your plan should also include a list of the _____ you will use, and your method. You should also include a _____ _____ to make sure your investigation is as safe as possible.

The measurements or observations you make are called _____. It is important that they are accurate and _____. The investigations should be repeatable and _____.

B Write a description for the following types of variable:

   a Independent variable _____

   b Dependent variable _____

   c Control variable _____

C Scientists classify data into three categories. Suggest an independent variable you could investigate for each type of data.

   a Continuous _____

   b Discrete _____

   c Categoric _____

D For each of the following statements, circle the correct word in **bold**.

The measurements you collect in an investigation are called **variables / data**.

Accurate / precise data is close to the true value of what you are trying to measure.

Accurate / precise data has a very small spread when measurements are repeated.

Data is **repeatable / reproducible** if you repeat the investigation several times and get similar results.

Data is **repeatable / reproducible** if someone else repeats the investigation and gets similar results.

E Which of the diagrams on the right could represent data that is not accurate but is precise?

_____

F A student sets light to a piece of magnesium ribbon.

Identify **one** risk and how it can be managed.

_____

_____

WS1.3 Recording data

A Fill in the gaps to complete the sentences.

Before starting an investigation you should produce a _____ table. You should put the

_____ variable in the first column, and allow space to take repeat _____ and calculate

a _____. Also remember to include _____ in the column headings. Check your data

for _____ – anomalous results, and _____ the measurement.

When plotting a graph, make sure you choose an appropriate _____ and put the independent

variable on the _____-axis. If both the dependent and independent variables are continuous, you

should plot a _____ _____. If your independent variable is categoric you should plot a

_____ _____. You can also display discrete or categoric data in a _____

_____.

B A group of students carried out an investigation to measure how far a toy car travels down slopes of different steepness, every 10° between 0° and 40°. They took repeat readings and calculated a mean.

Add headings, with units, to the table below to produce a results table for the students to collect their results.

C In the investigation in activity **B**, for a slope angle of 30° the students got the following distance readings:

60 cm   58 cm   80 cm

Circle the reading which is likely to be an **outlier**.

D Calculate the **mean** distance travelled from the data below, collected at a slope of 20°.

Distance ball travelled:	48 cm	50 cm	55 cm

_____ **cm**

E Sketch an appropriate graph in the space below, which would display all the data the students may have collected.

Hint: Include the data shown in activities **C** and **D**.

WS1.4 Analysing data

A Fill in the gaps to complete the sentences.

It is often helpful to plot _____ from an experiment, and draw a line of _____

_____ in order to analyse the results. This might be a straight line or a _____, and goes

as near as possible to as many points as possible. A _____ will state what was found out and any

_____ found between the variables, and use _____ knowledge to explain the pattern

and compare the results with the _____.

B Describe the pattern shown in the graph below.

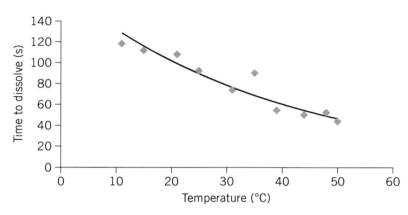

_____

_____

C a A student investigated the extension of a spring. The table shows the data obtained.

Draw a graph of the results below. Plot the data and draw a line of best fit, identifying and labelling any outliers.

Force (N)	Extension (cm)
1.0	0.5
2.0	1.0
3.0	1.4
4.0	1.8
5.0	2.3
6.0	3.8
7.0	3.3
8.0	3.7

b The student predicted that as force increased it would cause extension to increase. Write a **detailed** conclusion based on the data and your graph.

_____

_____

_____

_____

WS1.5 Evaluating data

A Fill in the gaps to complete the sentences.

There are two ways to _____ your investigation. You should discuss the _____

of the _____ that you have collected, and suggest and explain _____ to your

_____ so you can collect data of better quality if you repeat the experiment. Your suggested

improvements should increase the _____ that you have in your conclusion. Having few, or no,

_____ in the data increases the confidence in the conclusion. The spread of data tells you how

_____ the data is. Having a small spread in the data will give you _____ confidence

in your conclusion. _____ errors, such as a digital mass balance only reading to the nearest 1 g,

can increase the spread, or cause outliers. _____ errors, such as a newtonmeter reading 1 N even

when there is nothing attached, can reduce the accuracy. You might get better data by including a bigger

_____ of the independent variable, or taking _____ readings.

B Describe the stages in evaluating data from an experiment.

_____

_____

_____

C The table below shows repeated readings of force from two groups, for the same part of the same investigation.

Group One, force (N)	12, 17, 14
Group Two, force (N)	12, 15, 14, 14, 13

a Compare and contrast the data from the two groups, suggesting **two** reasons why the data may be different.

_____

_____

_____

_____

_____

b Explain two ways that group 1 could improve their data if they did the investigation again.

_____

_____

_____

Pinchpoint question

Answer the question below, then do the follow-up activity **with the same letter** as the answer you picked.

Roland and Amira wanted to find out the effect of light on the number of bubbles produced from a stem of pond weed. They took three measurements at each distance from the lamp.

Their results are shown in the table.

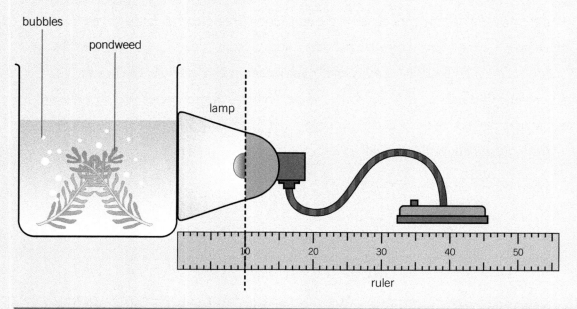

Distance from lamp (cm)	Number of oxygen bubbles produced in one minute			
	1st measurement	2nd measurement	3rd measurement	Mean
0	10	22	25	19
10	11	15	18	15
20	6	6	7	6
30	5	2	1	3
40	1	2	1	1

They conclude that the greater the distance from the lamp, the fewer bubbles are produced.

Which evaluation is best for these data?

We could increase our confidence in our conclusion by…

A changing one of the variables.

B repeating each measurement 5 times to reduce uncertainty in the results.

C increasing the number of readings by measuring at 5 cm intervals.

D trying to increase the spread of the results to improve precision.

Follow-up activities

A Draw a line to match each feature of investigation to its definition.

Type of feature

accurate	This describes a set of repeat measurements that are close together.
precise	When you take the measurements of an investigation again and get similar results.
repeatable	When other people carry out the same investigation and get similar measurements.
reproducible	Close to the true value of what you are measuring.

Definition

Hint: Make sure you know the difference between these key words. See WS1.2 Planning investigations and the Student Book Glossary for help.

B The table shows improvements that can made to a practical investigation.
Tick which improvements improve accuracy and which improve precision.

	Improvement	Accuracy	Precision
1	Change the measuring equipment to one that makes finer readings		
2	Aim to reduce the spread of results		
3	The same person takes the measurements		
4	Check the equipment is set to zero, e.g. a balance or forcemeter		
5	Repeat the measurements more often and remove the outliers		

Hint: Make sure you know the difference between the accuracy and precision. See WS1.2 Planning investigations and WS1.5 Evaluating data for help.

C a Suggest two reasons why counting gas bubbles can be inaccurate.

1 _____

2 _____

b Suggest a way to improve the accuracy of the experiment.

_____

_____

_____

Hint: See WS1.2 Planning investigations and WS1.5 Evaluating data for help.

D Tick the ways in which you could change the investigation to get better data.

1   Get someone else to do the experiment ☐

2   Take readings more often, e.g. every 5 cm instead of every 10 cm ☐

3   Change one of the variables, e.g. the type of pond weed ☐

4   Take more readings, e.g. 5 readings instead of 3 ☐

5   Use more accurate apparatus, e.g. gas syringes to measure volume of gas ☐

6   Identify outliers ☐

Hint: Focus on improving the data you collect. See WS1.5 Evaluating data for help.

 Pinchpoint review

Now look back at the question – do you think you chose the right letter?
Turn to the Answers page to find out.

B1.1 Observing cells

A Fill in the gaps below to complete the sentences.

All living organisms are made up of _____ – these are the building blocks of life. To see cells in detail

you need to use a _____. This _____ the object. Looking carefully and in detail at an

object is called making an _____.

B A light microscope is used to magnify objects.

Match each missing label on the diagram to the correct word below.
Write **W**, **X**, **Y**, or **Z** beside each word.

slide ☐   eyepiece lens ☐

objective lens ☐   light ☐

C Henry wants to observe a leaf under the microscope. He takes a small piece of leaf and places it on a microscope slide. He places the slide on the stage of the microscope.

a Describe what he should do next to observe the leaf.

_____

_____

_____

b Explain how Henry could observe the leaf in greater detail.

_____

c Henry observed the leaf using an eye piece lens of ×10 magnification and an objective lens of ×50 magnification.
Calculate the total magnification he used.

_____

B1.2 Plant and animal cells

A Fill in the gaps below to complete the sentences.

Plant and animal cells both contain a _____ that controls the cell, _____ where

chemical reactions take place, a _____ _____ that controls what comes in and out

of the cell and _____ where respiration occurs. Plant cells also contain a rigid _____

_____ that provides support, _____ for photosynthesis and a _____

that contains cell sap to keep the cell firm.

B Label the main components in the animal and plant cells below.

C List four components found in **both** animal and plant cells, and describe their functions:

	Component	Function
1	_____	_____
2	_____	_____
3	_____	_____
4	_____	_____

D Explain the function of the following plant cell components.

a Chloroplasts

_____

b Vacuole

_____

c Cell wall

_____

E Name the fibre that makes up plant cell walls.

_____

B1.3 Specialised cells

A Fill in the gaps to complete the sentences.

Some cells have special features to carry out their functions. These cells are called _____ cells.

For example, in animals, _____ _____ cells have haemoglobin for carrying oxygen,

and nerve cells are long and thin to carry electrical _____. _____ cells have a head

and tail so they can carry male genetic material to the female egg. In plants, root _____ cells have

a large surface area to absorb _____ and nutrients from the soil and leaf cells are packed with

_____ to carry out photosynthesis.

B Name each type of specialised cell described below:

  a Contains genetic information from the female parent _____

  b Transmits electrical impulses around your body _____

  c Packed with chloroplasts to maximise photosynthesis _____

C Circle **true** or **false** for the following statements about red blood cells.

For incorrect statements, correct the sentence so that it is true.

  a They carry oxygen around the body.   **true / false**

  b They have a nucleus.   **true / false**

  c They have a disc-like shape.   **true / false**

  d They contain chlorophyll.   **true / false**

D This is a sperm cell.

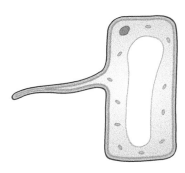

Explain why it has the following features.

  a Tail: _____

  b Lots of mitochondria: _____

  c Streamlined head: _____

E Identify this specialised cell and explain how it is adapted to its function.

_____

_____

B1.4 Movement of substances

A Fill in the gaps to complete the sentences.

Substances move from an area where they are in a _____ concentration to an area where they are

in a _____ concentration. This process is called _____. Many substances move into

and out of your cells by using this process. For example in gas exchange, _____ diffuses into your

cells from the blood and _____ diffuses out of your cells into the blood, so that it can be taken to the

lungs and breathed out.

B Many substances move into and out of your cells by diffusion.

List **two** substances that diffuse **into** your cells from the blood.

1 _____   **2** _____

C Two different liquids were placed in a container (**A**).

Complete the diagram to show how the molecules have moved after 10 seconds (**B**), and after 2 minutes, (**C**), as a
result of diffusion.

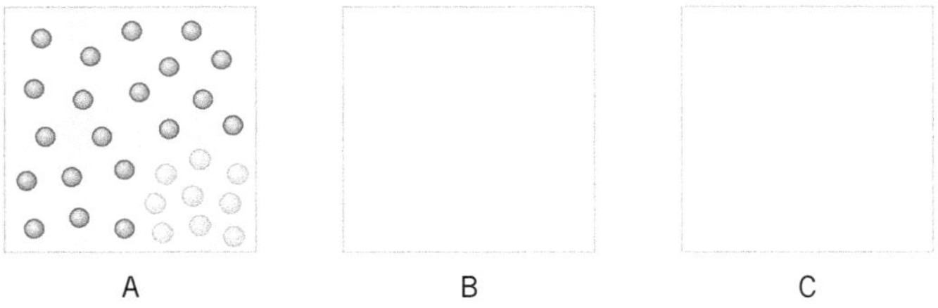

A   B   C

D Explain how water moves into a plant from the soil.

_____

_____

_____

E If a plant is not watered regularly it will wilt.

Explain how watering the plant will enable the plant to stand upright.

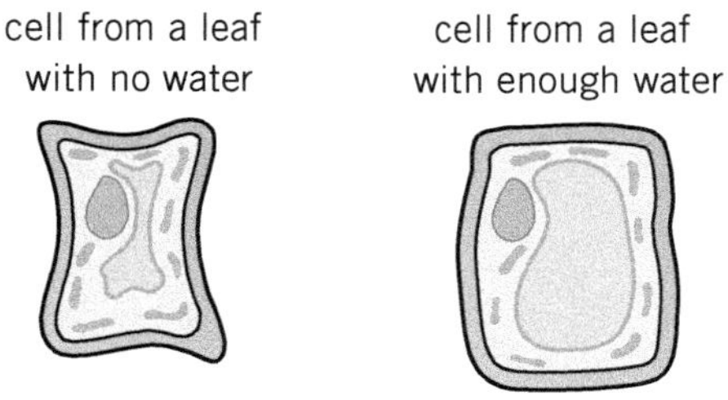

cell from a leaf   cell from a leaf
with no water   with enough water

Hint: Use the information in the diagram to help you.

_____

_____

_____

_____

B1.5 Unicellular organisms

A Fill in the gaps to complete the sentences.

Amoebas and _____ are examples of _____ organisms. This means that they consist

of only _____ cell. Both organisms have a cell membrane filled with _____ and

contain a nucleus. Euglenas also have _____, which make them look green, an _____

_____ which detects light, and a _____ so they can 'swim'.

B Unicellular organisms reproduce by binary fission to produce two identical cells.

Describe the **two** main steps in this process.

Step 1 _____

Step 2 _____

C This is a euglena. It lives in fresh water.

Give the function of the:

a Flagella _____

b Chloroplasts _____

c Eye spot _____

D Euglenas have chloroplasts but they are not plants. Explain why.

_____

_____

E Amoebas cannot photosynthesise. Explain how they take in food.

_____

_____

_____

13

Pinchpoint question

Answer the question below, then do the follow-up activity **with the same letter** as the answer you picked.

Which of the following best describes the process of diffusion?

A The movement of particles from an area of high concentration to an area of low concentration.

B The process plants use to suck water into their roots.

C The random movement of particles from low to high concentration.

D The process by which water molecules move into a cell.

Follow-up activities

A The data in the table show how the surface area affects how quickly diffusion can take place:

Surface area (cm²)	10	20	30	40	50
Diffusion rate (arbitrary units)	2	4	6	8	10

Explain why many body cells are adapted to have a large surface area.

Hint: Think about what your body needs to survive. For further help see B1 1.4 Movement of substances.

_____

_____

_____

B Look at the diagram and explain what is happening.

Use the following words in your explanation:

because	diffuse	concentration

Hint: Start your answer by explaining why water molecules move into the first cell.
For further help see B1 1.4 Movement of substances.

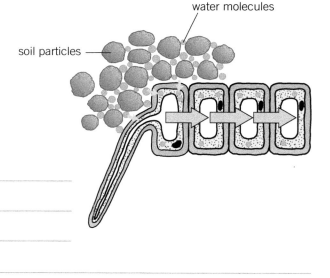

_____

_____

_____

_____

C This diagram shows how you smell burnt toast in another room.

a In each row, if there is a difference in concentration, circle the box with the highest concentration of 'burnt-toast smell' particles.

Hint: Highest concentration = area where there are the most particles. For further help see B1 1.4 Movement of substances.

Kitchen	Hallway	Living room
toast burns		

• grey dots = air particles   • black dots = 'burnt-toast smell' particles

b Now complete the following sentences.

The particles that make up the smell of burnt toast move from a place of _____ concentration

to a place of _____ concentration. Diffusion continues until there is the _____

concentration of 'burnt-toast smell' particles everywhere.

D The plant cell in the first diagram was placed into salt water that had a very low concentration of water. After a few minutes the cell looked like the second diagram.

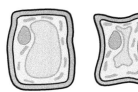

a Add an arrow to the first picture to show the direction of the movement of water molecules.

b Write a sentence explaining why water moves into or out of the cell.

Hint: Where was the highest concentration of water molecules at the start of the experiment? For further help see B1 1.4.

_____

_____

_____

⊗ **Pinchpoint review**

Now look back at the question – do you think you chose the right letter?
Turn to the Answers page to find out.

B2.1 Levels of organisation

A Fill in the gaps to complete the sentences.

_____ organisms have five levels of organisation. This is called a _____ . Cells are the building blocks of life. Groups of similar cells working together are called _____ and different tissues working together are called an _____ . A group of different organs that work together is called an _____ _____ . Finally, an _____ is made up of a number of organ systems working together to perform all the processes needed to stay alive.

B Describe what is meant by each of the following key terms:

a Tissue _____

b Organ _____

c Organ system _____

C Organise the following into a hierarchy, starting with the smallest, and list the level of organisation it belongs to.

dog	circulatory system	blood	heart	red blood cell

Structure	Level of organisation
_____	_____
_____	_____
_____	_____
_____	_____
_____	_____

D Other than blood, name a type of a tissue found in the heart and describe its function.

_____

_____

E Flowers contain both male and female sex organs.

a Name the level of organisation that flowers belong to.

_____

b Describe the main function of flowers.

_____

_____

_____

B2.2 Gas exchange

A Fill in the gaps to complete the sentences.

Breathing is carried out by the _____ system and the major organs of this system

are your _____. When you inhale you take in _____ and when you

_____ you give out carbon dioxide. When you inhale, air travels in through your

mouth and nose and then through your _____. It then travels into your lungs through

the _____ and then through a bronchiole, finally moving into an air sac called an

_____. These have thin walls and create a large surface area for _____

_____, which means that the gases can diffuse in and out of the blood easily.

B Label the diagram of the human respiratory system.

C There are millions of alveoli in the lungs. Explain how they are adapted for gas exchange.

_____

_____

_____

D These pie charts show the difference in composition of inhaled and exhaled air.

other gases 1%   carbon dioxide CO_2 0.04%   oxygen O_2 20.96%   nitrogen N_2 78%   inhaled air

other gases 2%   carbon dioxide CO_2 4%   oxygen O_2 16%   nitrogen N_2 78%   exhaled air

Use the data to describe and explain the differences between the gases in inhaled and exhaled air.

a Carbon dioxide _____

_____

b Oxygen _____

_____

c Nitrogen _____

_____

B2.3 Breathing

A Fill in the gaps to complete the sentences.

When you inhale, the muscles between your _____ and your diaphragm _____.

This _____ the volume of your chest cavity which _____ the pressure, causing

air to be drawn in. When you exhale, the muscles _____; this _____ the volume

of your chest cavity. This _____ the pressure and forces air _____. You can use a

_____ to model this process. Smoking and diseases such as _____ can reduce

lung _____.

B Explain how the actions of the ribcage and diaphragm cause you to inhale.

_____

_____

_____

_____

C A bell jar model can be used to model what happens during breathing.

a Describe how the model can be used to represent what happens when you exhale.

_____

_____

_____

b Describe **one** limitation of this model.

_____

D Explain how you can use the equipment shown to measure your lung volume.

_____

_____

_____

_____

B2.4 Skeleton

A Fill in the gaps to complete the sentences.

Your _____ is made up of bones. The skeleton has four functions: to _____ your organs,

to _____ the body, to help you _____, and to make red and white _____

cells. These cells are made in bone _____, which is found in the centre of some bones.

B Together all the bones in your body make up your skeleton.

Label the missing bones on the diagram.

C Describe how the skeleton enables you to move. Include the terms **muscles** and **joints** in your answer.

_____

_____

_____

_____

D Describe **three** functions of the skeleton, other than movement.

1 _____

2 _____

3 _____

E Give an example of a bone and the organ it protects.

Bone _____   Organ _____

B2.5 Movement: joints

A Fill in the gaps to complete the sentences.

_____ are where bones join together. Different types of joint allow _____

in different _____ . Bones are held together in a joint by _____ . The

ends of bones in a joint are covered with _____ to stop them rubbing together. When

a muscle _____ it exerts a _____ on a bone, which is measured in

_____ (N), and it pulls the muscle in a certain direction. This is called biomechanics.

B Different joints allow movement in different directions.

   a Describe the difference in movement in the knee and shoulder joints. Use the terms **ball and socket** and **hinge**.

_____

_____

   b Explain why the joints in the skull are unusual.

_____

_____

C You can carry out simple experiments to measure the force of different body muscles. Explain how you could measure the force of your triceps muscle (the muscle in the back of your arm).

_____

_____

_____

D **a** Label the parts of the knee joint in the diagram below.

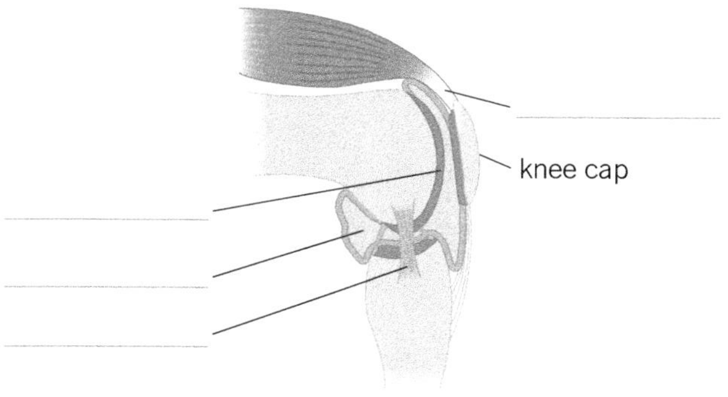

knee cap

   b Describe the function of the following parts of the knee joint.

Tendon _____

Ligament _____

Cartilage _____

Fluid _____

   c Name the part of the bone that produces blood cells. _____

B2.6 Movement: muscles

A Fill in the gaps to complete the sentences.

Muscles are attached to bones by _____. When a muscle contracts it _____ and

pulls on a _____. Pairs of _____ work together at a _____ to cause

movement. These are called _____ muscles. As one muscle in the pair contracts the other muscle

_____.

B Muscles have a range of functions in the body.

Describe the main function of the muscles in the:

a heart _____

b intestine _____

c leg _____

C Describe what is meant by the term 'antagonistic muscles'.

_____

_____

_____

D The diagram shows a leg and four of the major muscles involved in movement: A, B, C, and D.

With reference to the muscle pairs labelled A–D, explain how:

a the knee bends.

_____

_____

b toes point upwards.

_____

_____

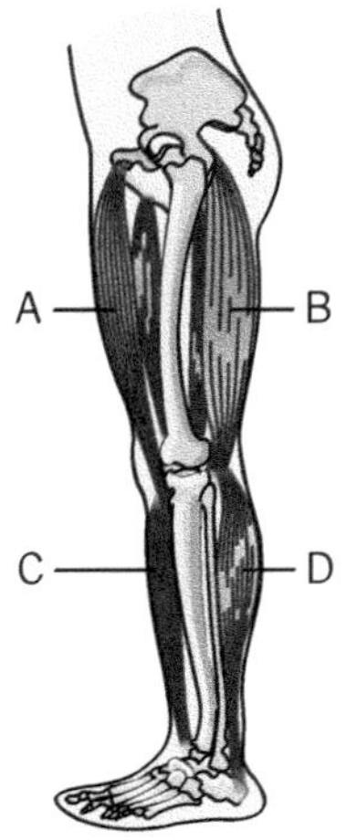

E Describe what is meant by the term 'muscle fatigue'.

_____

_____

Pinchpoint question

Answer the question below, then do the follow-up activity **with the same letter** as the answer you picked.

Which shape is most suited for gas exchange?

A Shape A as it has a smaller surface area

B Shape B as It has a larger surface area

C Either shape as they have the same surface area

D Either shape as they have the same volume

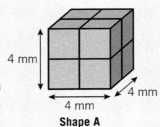

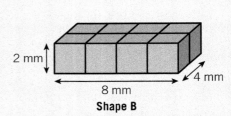

Shape A

Shape B

Follow-up activities

A During gas exchange, oxygen diffuses from your lungs into your blood through the alveoli.

Look back at the diagram in the question at the top of this page. Imagine that one molecule of oxygen could diffuse from each surface square of the shape, at the same time.

Use the table below to calculate how many molecules of oxygen are diffusing at the same time.

Hint: If you find it difficult to visualise the shapes, use a real 3D shape such as your rubber or pencil case to help. For further help see B1 2.2 Gas exchange.

Faces	Shape A	Shape B
Top and bottom	$2 \times 4 = 8$	
Front (facing you) and back		
Left and right		
Total		

B Useful nutrients diffuse into your blood from your small intestine. To maximise this exchange, your small intestine is covered in finger-like projections called villi.

Suggest how villi help the process of nutrient absorption.

Hint: The villi in your intestine work in a similar way to the alveoli in your lungs. For further help see B1 2.2 Gas exchange and B1 1.4 Movement of substances.

C The surface area of shape A is 96 mm².

    a Calculate the surface area of shape B.

Hint: To calculate the surface area, you need to work out the area of each face of the cuboid by multiplying its length by its width. Then add the area of all the faces together. Some people find it easier to draw out the net of the shape first: you can use the one shown below. For further help see B1 2.2 Gas exchange.

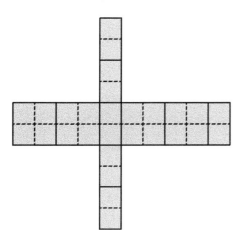

_____ mm²

    b Now complete the following sentence by circling the correct term.

       The surface area of shape B is **bigger than / smaller than / the same as** shape A.

D Water is placed into two containers, A and B, which have the same volume. Container A represents a narrow, deep puddle and container B represents a shallow, wide puddle. They are placed outside on a sunny day.

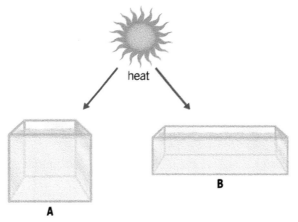

Complete the following sentences by circling the correct term in each sentence.

As the Sun shines on the puddle, the water will **diffuse / condense / evaporate**.

The surface area of container A exposed to the Sun is **the same as / larger than / smaller than** that of container B.

Therefore puddle **A / B** will disappear faster even though they have the same volume.

Hint: Think about which puddle will be affected most by the heat from the Sun. For further help see B1 2.2 Gas exchange.

 Pinchpoint review

    Now look back at the question – do you think you chose the right letter?
    Turn to the Answers page to find out.

B3.1 Adolescence

A Fill in the gaps to complete the sentences.

The period of time when a person develops from a child into an adult is known as _____.

The _____ changes that take place are called _____. These changes are caused by _____ _____. Both males and females grow _____ and get _____ hair. Boys' voices _____ and their _____ widen.

Girls will start their _____ and their _____ widen.

B Describe the difference between adolescence and puberty.

_____

_____

_____

C Girls and boys undergo a number of **physical** changes during puberty.

Describe the main changes that occur – in boys, girls, or both – using the table below.

Boys	Girls

D Explain why the following changes take place during puberty.

a Girls' hips widen.

_____

_____

b Girls develop breasts.

_____

_____

B3.2 Reproductive system

A Fill in the gaps to complete the sentences.

The function of the male reproductive system is to make _____ cells and release them inside a female's _____. Sperm are made in the _____, which are contained in the scrotum. They then pass through the _____ _____ and urethra, and are then released from the _____ during sexual intercourse. The function of the female reproductive system is to release _____ cells from the ovaries. An egg passes through the _____ to the _____. If a pregnancy occurs, this is where a baby grows and develops.

B Label the main structures of the female reproductive system on the diagram below.

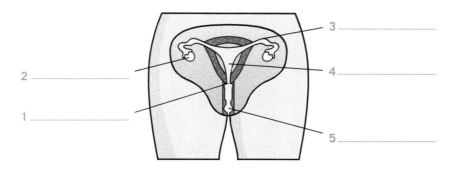

C Label the main structures of the male reproductive system on the diagram below.

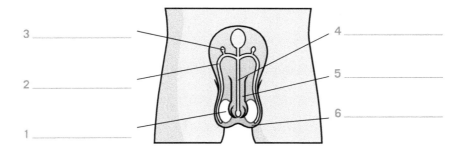

D Describe the function of the following structures.

  a Ovary_____
  b Cervix_____
  c Vagina_____

E Explain how sperm is made and released from the male body.

Include the following terms in your answer:

glands	penis	semen	sperm duct	testes	urethra

_____

_____

_____

_____

B3.3 Fertilisation and implantation

A Fill in the gaps to complete the sentences.

_____ are reproductive cells. The male gamete is called a _____ cell and the female gamete is called an _____ cell. Every month an egg is released from an _____ and wafted along the oviduct by tiny hairs called _____. During sexual intercourse, sperm are released into the vagina. This is known as _____. The sperm swim towards the egg in the oviduct. To create a new organism the _____ of the sperm and egg cell need to join together. This is called _____. The fertilised egg then divides to form a ball of cells called an _____. The embryo attaches to the lining of the _____ and begins to develop into a baby. This is called _____.

B Describe the process of fertilisation.

_____

_____

C Complete the following table to compare the male and female gametes.

	Male	Female
Name of gamete		
Where is it made?		
Which tube is it released into?		
How does it move?		

D Complete the flow diagram to show the structures in the female body that the sperm passes through in order to fertilise an egg.

Sperm released from penis → [ ] → [ ] → [ ] → [ ]

E Describe what happens to the fertilised egg after fertilisation.

_____

_____

_____

A Fill in the gaps to complete the sentences.

The period of time an organism develops in the _____ is known as _____. In humans this is about _____ months. The fetus develops inside a fluid _____. This protects the fetus from any bumps. During this time the fetus receives nutrients and _____ from the mother. These pass from the mother's blood to the fetus's _____ in the _____. The fetus is connected to the placenta by the _____ _____. During birth the mother's _____ relaxes and the _____ wall contracts, pushing the baby out of the body through the _____.

B Describe briefly what happens during gestation.

_____

_____

C After eight weeks of growth, the embryo is called a fetus. Label the main structures in the diagram below.

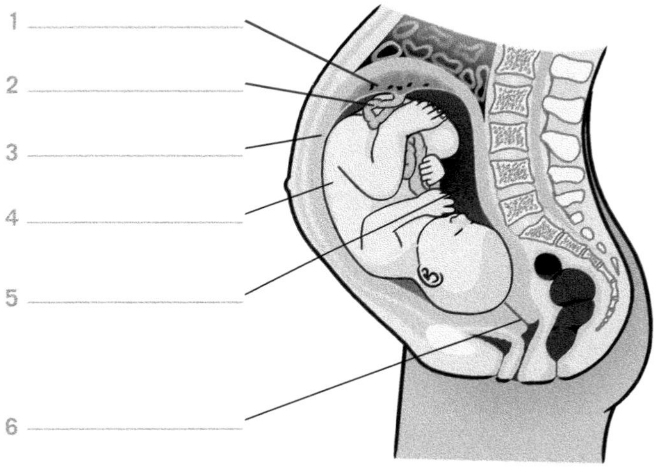

1 _____

2 _____

3 _____

4 _____

5 _____

6 _____

D Explain the function the following structures perform during gestation.

a Placenta

_____

_____

b Fluid sac

_____

_____

E With reference to contractions, explain what happens during birth.

_____

_____

_____

B3.5 The menstrual cycle

A Fill in the gaps to complete the sentences.

The female reproductive system works in a cycle called the ______________ cycle. Each month an ______________ is released. This is called ______________. If this is not fertilised the uterus ______________ breaks down and leaves the body. This is called a ______________. The cycle then begins again.

B Add labels to the diagram below to indicate when the main events in the menstrual cycle occur.

DAY:	**0 / 1**	**5**	**10**	**15**	**20**	**25**	**28**

C **a** Describe what happens to the uterus lining if the egg is **not** fertilised.

____

____

b Describe what happens to the uterus lining if the egg **is** fertilised.

____

____

____

D For **two** named methods of contraception, explain how they prevent pregnancy.

Method 1 ______________

Explanation ______________________________

Method 2 ______________

Explanation ______________________________

B3.6 Flowers and pollination

A Fill in the gaps to complete the sentences.

Pollination is the name given to the transfer of _____ from the _____ to the stigma. Pollen can be carried by the wind or by _____ . To attract insects, flowers are often _____ coloured, contain _____ and are _____ smelling. Wind-pollinated plants produce _____ amounts of _____ pollen. Their anthers and _____ hang outside the flower.

B Complete the labels of the flower structures on the diagram.

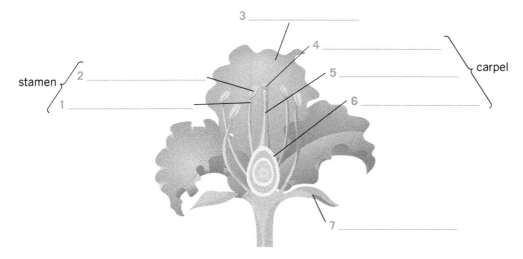

C Describe the process of pollination.

_____

_____

D Tulips are pollinated by insects. Explain **three** ways the flower is adapted for this type of pollination.

1 _____

2 _____

3 _____

E Explain the differences in the types of pollen produced by insect-pollinated and wind-pollinated plants.

_____

_____

_____

B3.7 Fertilisation and germination

A Fill in the gaps to complete the sentences.

During ______________, the nucleus of the ______________ grain and the ______________ join together. The ovary then develops into the ______________ and the ovules become ______________.

To grow a new plant, the seed needs to ______________. For this to occur it needs ______________, water, and oxygen.

B Label the diagram below, showing the main structures involved in fertilisation.

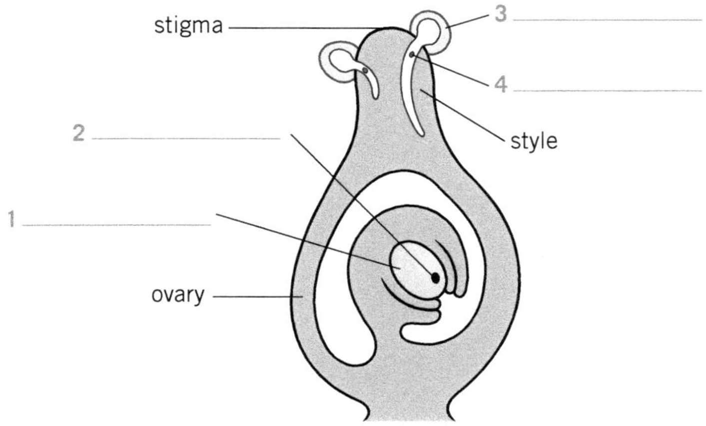

stigma
3 ______________
4 ______________
style
2 ______________
1 ______________
ovary

C Describe the processes that occur after pollination, including fertilisation and seed formation.

____

____

____

____

D Complete the flow diagram to explain the main steps in germination. Use the key words:

shoot	seed coat	root	light

1 Seed absorbs water rapidly – ______________

↓

2 ______________

↓

3 ______________

↓

4 First leaf appears – ______________

Hint: For help with this activity, look back at the germination diagram in B3.7 of the Student Book.

E A student planted 25 seeds, but only 18 of the seeds germinated.

Calculate the percentage of seeds that germinated.

______________ %

B3.8 Seed dispersal

A Fill in the gaps to complete the sentences.

Seeds are _____ away from the parent plant to reduce _____. This increases their

chances of survival as they have more _____ and nutrients to grow. Seeds can be dispersed by the

_____, explosion, _____, and water.

B Name the method of seed dispersal used by the following seeds and describe how the seed is adapted to its method of dispersal.

a

Method _____

Adaptation _____

_____

_____

_____

b

Method _____

Adaptation _____

_____

_____

_____

C Explain why seeds are dispersed.

_____

_____

D A group of students carried out an investigation to see if seeds with larger wings travel further when blown by a fan.

a Write a suitable hypothesis for this investigation.

_____

_____

_____

b Identify the types of variable used in their investigation. Include the units of measurement in your answers.

i independent variable _____

ii dependent variable _____

iii control variable _____

Pinchpoint question

Answer the question below, then do the follow-up activity **with the same letter** as the answer you picked.

Which of the following statements best describes fertilisation in organisms?

A   Fusion of nuclei of male and female gametes

B   Process required to make a baby

C   Transfer of pollen from anther to stigma

D   When male and female cells meet

Follow-up activities

A   Look at the diagram of a flower.

Explain how this plant is adapted to increase the chances of pollination and describe the process of seed formation. Include the word **fertilisation** in your answer.

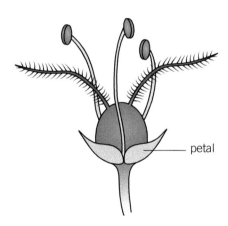

petal

Hint: Is this a wind-pollinated or insect-pollinated plant? For further help see B1 3.6 Flowers and pollination.

_____

_____

_____

_____

B   Complete the table with appropriate words to compare fertilisation in plants and animals.

Hint: Gamete is the proper name for a sex cell. For further help see B1 3.3 Fertilisation and implantation and B1 3.6 Flowers and pollination.

	Animal	Plant
Male gamete		
Female gamete		
What happens during fertilisation?		
Where does fertilisation occur?		
What develops as a result of fertilisation?		

C In order to make a seed, both pollination and fertilisation need to occur. Read the statements and write down the order you think will give the best description.

Hint: Pollination has to occur first and is helped by insects or wind. For further help see B1 3.7 Fertilisation and germination.

Correct order ☐ ☐ ☐ ☐ ☐ ☐

1 Pollen nucleus travels down tube.

2 This is called fertilisation.

3 Pollen nucleus fuses with ovule nuclei.

4 This is called pollination.

5 Pollen from the anther is transferred to the stigma.

6 The pollen grain grows a tube down the style and into an ovule in the ovary.

D Add a caption under each picture to describe the steps which take place to allow fertilisation to occur.

Hint: Use the terms pollen tube, pollen nucleus, ovule nucleus. For further help see B1 3.7 Fertilisation and germination.

1 stigma —— pollen grain
—— style

ovule nucleus
ovule
ovary

2

3

_____

_____

_____

_____

Pinchpoint review
Now look back at the question – do you think you chose the right letter?
Turn to the Answers page to find out.

B1 Revision questions

1 🧪🧪 **Figure 1** shows a flower.

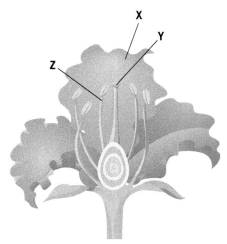

Figure 1

a Name the structures **X**, **Y**, and **Z**.   (*3 marks*)

  X _____

  Y _____

  Z _____

b Pollen and ovules are the plant gametes.

  i Define the word **gamete**.   (*1 mark*)

    _____

  ii Name the part of the flower where pollen is made.
                              (*1 mark*)

    _____

  iii Name the part of the flower where ovules are found.   (*1 mark*)

    _____

c Give **two** different ways in which a plant can be pollinated and give an example of a plant which is pollinated by each method.   (*2 marks*)

  1 _____ **example:** _____

  2 _____ **example:** _____

d To produce a seed, fertilisation must occur.

  Describe what happens during the process of fertilisation.   (*2 marks*)

  _____

  _____

  _____

2 🧪🧪 Plant and animal cells contain smaller structures.

a Draw a line from each plant cell structure to its correct function.   (*3 marks*)

nucleus	stores sap and helps to keep the cell firm
vacuole	controls the activities of the cell
cytoplasm	where the cell's chemical reactions take place

b Explain why plant cells contain chloroplasts.
                                  (*1 mark*)

  _____

  _____

3 🧪🧪 A group of students wanted to observe some onion cells under a microscope.

a Explain how the students should set up and use the microscope so they can view the cells clearly.   (*6 marks*)

  _____

  _____

  _____

  _____

  _____

  _____

  _____

  _____

  _____

  _____

  _____

  _____

b Sketch a diagram below, showing what you would expect the students to see through the microscope. Label **three** cell components.   (*4 marks*)

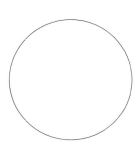

c Plant cells have a cell wall.

i Write down what cell walls are made from.

(1 mark)

_____

ii Explain the function of the cell wall. *(2 marks)*

_____

_____

4 🧪🧪 **Figure 2** shows a structure found in your lungs

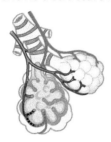

Figure 2

a Name the structure that forms the gas exchange surface. *(1 mark)*

_____

b Describe this structure's role in gas exchange.

(2 marks)

_____

_____

_____

c Explain how this structure is adapted to perform its function. *(3 marks)*

_____

_____

_____

_____

5 🧪🧪 A student measured his lung volume using the equipment shown in **Figure 3**.

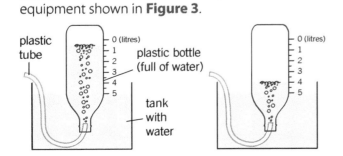

Figure 3

a Calculate the volume of air exhaled by the student.

(2 marks)

_____ litres

b Write down **two** differences between the air exhaled by the student, and the air inhaled. *(2 marks)*

1 _____

2 _____

c Suggest **one** factor that could reduce the student's lung volume. *(1 mark)*

_____

6 🧪🧪 Hermione measured the force of her triceps muscle by pushing down onto a set of bathroom scales, measuring the force in newtons. **Table 1** shows her results.

Table 1

Force measurement 1 (N)	Force measurement 2 (N)	Force measurement 3 (N)
450	410	370

a Calculate the mean force from Hermione's triceps muscle. Remember to state the units. *(3 marks)*

_____

_____

b Suggest **one** reason why each force measurement was different. *(1 mark)*

_____

_____

c The biceps and triceps muscles are found in the upper arm, as shown in **Figure 4**.

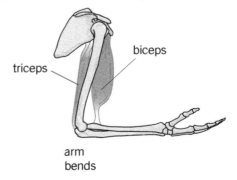

Figure 4

Explain how these muscles work together to move your lower arm upwards and downwards. *(3 marks)*

_____

_____

_____

_____

7 🧪🧪 Basil is an edible plant. A group of students were asked to investigate the conditions needed for basil seeds to germinate. They placed seeds onto cotton wool, in the conditions shown in **Figure 5**.

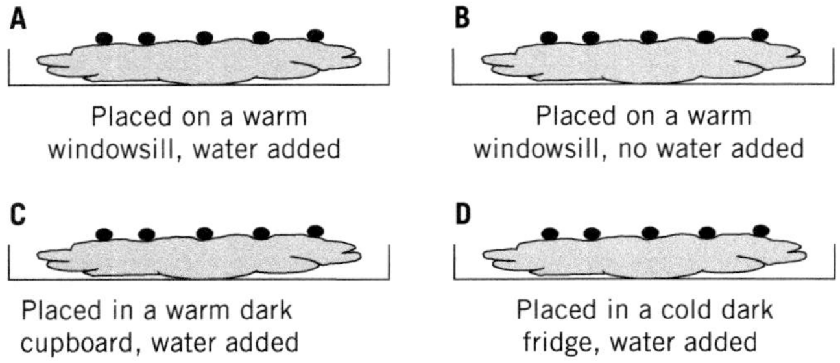

A — Placed on a warm windowsill, water added

B — Placed on a warm windowsill, no water added

C — Placed in a warm dark cupboard, water added

D — Placed in a cold dark fridge, water added

Figure 5

a Circle each dish where you would expect germination to occur. *(2 marks)*

b The students used a total of 20 seeds. Only 8 of these germinated.

Calculate the percentage of seeds that germinated. *(2 marks)*

_____%

c Basil seeds have a sticky outer layer, called mucilage. Suggest and explain how basil seeds are dispersed. *(2 marks)*

_____

_____

_____

_____

8 🧪🧪🧪 Susan has arthritis in her knee. An ultrasound scan showed that Susan had lost some cartilage in her knee joint.

Suggest and explain the symptoms she is likely to have. *(4 marks)*

_____

_____

_____

_____

9 🧪🧪🧪 A couple wish to have a baby.

a When is the most likely time in a woman's menstrual cycle for her to get pregnant?

Days 1 → 3 ☐   Days 14 → 16 ☐

Days 24 → 26 ☐   *(1 mark)*

b Explain your answer. *(2 marks)*

_____

_____

c Explain how sexual intercourse can lead to a fertilised egg implanting in the uterus. *(6 marks)*

_____

_____

_____

_____

_____

_____

_____

_____

d Explain **one** way pregnancy can be prevented. *(2 marks)*

_____

_____

_____

10 🧪🧪🧪 **Figure 6** shows a drawing of a flower.

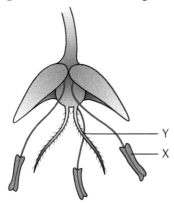

Figure 6

a Identify structures X and Y.

X _____ (*1 mark*)

Y _____ (*1 mark*)

b Use information in the diagram and your own knowledge to explain how this flower is pollinated.

(*4 marks*)

_____

_____

_____

_____

_____

11 🧪🧪🧪 A group of students observed some pond-water organisms under the microscope. They placed a droplet of water containing *Daphnia* on a special slide as shown in **Figure 7**.

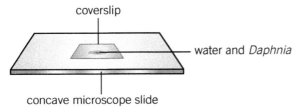

coverslip

water and *Daphnia*

concave microscope slide

Figure 7

a Suggest **one** reason why they added water.

(*1 mark*)

_____

b **Figure 8** shows what they observed using a ×10 eyepiece lens and a ×4 objective lens.

Figure 8

i Calculate the total magnification used.

(*1 mark*)

_____ %

ii Use information in the diagram to explain how the students knew they were looking at a multicellular organism. (*2 marks*)

_____

_____

_____

c The students could see the heart of the *Daphnia* beating.

i Explain how they could observe the heart in more detail. (*1 mark*)

_____

ii Name **one** type of specialised cell they would expect to find in this organ and explain its function. (*2 marks*)

_____

_____

iii Explain the function of **three** components you would expect to find in this cell. (*3 marks*)

_____

_____

_____

_____

_____

_____

B1 Checklist

Revision question	Outcome	Topic reference	🙁	😐	🙂
1a	Identify the main structures in a flower.	B1 3.6			
1b	State the definition of 'gamete'.	B1 3.3			
	State the function of parts of a flower.	B1 3.6			
1c	Name two different ways in which a plant can be pollinated.	B1 3.6			
1d	Describe the process of fertilisation.	B1 3.7			
2a	Match some components of a cell to their functions.	B1 1.2			
2b	State the function of chloroplasts.	B1 1.2			
3a	Describe how to use a microscope to observe a cell.	B1 1.1			
3b	Sketch a plant cell as it would appear through a microscope.	B1 1.2			
3c	Describe the function of cell components.	B1 1.2			
4a	Identify structures in the gas exchange system.	B1 2.2			
4b	Describe the role of the alveoli in gas exchange.	B1 2.2			
4c	Describe how parts of the gas exchange system are adapted to their function.	B1 2.2			
5a	Calculate lung volume from experimental data.	B1 2.3			
5b	Describe the differences between inhaled and exhaled air.	B1 2.2			
5c	Suggest factors which could affect lung volume.	B1 2.3			
6a	Calculate a mean average.	WS1.3			
		B1 2.5			
6b	Suggest reasons for variation in experimental data.	WS1.5			
		B1 2.5			
6c	Explain how muscles work together to produce movement.	B1 2.6			
7a	Describe the conditions required for seed germination.	B1 3.7			
7b	Calculate a percentage from experimental data.	B1 3.7			
7c	Describe methods of seed dispersal.	B1 3.8			
8	Explain how the parts of a joint allow it to function.	B1 2.5			
9a, b	Describe the stages of the menstrual cycle.	B1 3.5			
9c	Explain how the male and female reproductive systems work together to result in pregnancy.	B1 3.3			
9d	Explain how contraception can be used to prevent pregnancy.	B1 3.5			
10a	Identify the main structures in an unknown flower.	B1 3.6			
10b	Explain how the structures in a flower are adapted for pollination.	B1 3.6			
11a	Select appropriate experimental apparatus.	WS1.2			
11bi	Calculate magnification used to observe an organism.	B1 1.1			
11bii	Explain what a unicellular organism is.	B1 1.5			
11ci	Explain how to use a microscope to observe structures in more detail.	B1 1.1			
11cii	Describe examples of specialised animal cells.	B1 1.3			
11ciii	Explain the function of cell components.	B1 1.2			

C1.1 The particle model

A Fill in the gaps to complete the sentences.

Materials are made up of tiny _____. Many materials are mixtures of different substances. Different

substances are made from _____ particles. The properties of a substance describe what it

_____ like and how it _____. Every substance has its own properties, which depend on

what its particles are like, how its particles are _____, and how its particles _____ around.

B The table gives some information about particles in four substances. The diagrams show how the particles are arranged in solid gold and silver.

Substance	Radius of particle (nm)	Relative mass of particle
gold	0.144	197
hafnium	0.157	178
silver	0.144	108
zirconium	0.157	91

gold   silver

Choose data from the table to explain why a 1 cm³ cube of gold has a greater mass than a 1 cm³ cube of silver. You will need to refer to the diagrams in your answer.

_____

_____

_____

_____

C The particles in solid hafnium and solid zirconium are arranged in the same way.

a Choose data from the table in activity **B** to predict which has the greater mass. Underline your answer: **1 cm³ cube of hafnium / 1 cm³ cube of zirconium**

b Explain your prediction.

_____

_____

_____

D A student uses spheres to model liquid gold and liquid silver. The diagrams show her models. Evaluate how the student's model:

a helps to explain why you can pour liquid gold.

_____

_____

b helps to explain why 1 cm³ of gold has a greater mass than 1 cm³ of silver.

beaker

10 g metal sphere to represent a gold particle

A model of liquid gold

A model of liquid silver

beaker

2 g plastic sphere to represent a silver particle

_____

_____

c is different from real liquid gold and real liquid silver.

_____

C1.2 States of matter

A Fill in the gaps to complete the sentences.

Most substances can exist in the solid state, the liquid state, and the _____ state. These are the three

states of _____. The particles of a substance in each of its three states are the same. In each of the

three states of matter, the arrangement and _____ of the particles are _____.

B Tick one or more columns next to each property to show the possible state or states of the substance.

Property of substance	The substance could be in the ...		
	solid state	liquid state	gas state
Can be compressed			
Can be poured			
Has a fixed shape			

C Use the particle model to explain each observation below. Each explanation should be one short sentence only.

   a   A solid has a fixed shape.

   _____

   b   A liquid cannot be compressed.

   _____

   c   A gas flows.

   _____

D Liquid water changes to the solid state when it is cooled to 0 °C.
Complete the table to compare the properties of water at 10 °C and at −10 °C.
You need to write just **yes** or **no** in each column.

	at 10 °C?	at −10 °C?
Can water be compressed …		
Does water take the shape of the bottom of its container …		
Does water flow …		

E Two students are talking about sand.

You can pour sand, so it is liquid.

You cannot compress sand, so it is solid.

Hannah

Brooke

   a   Write down the name of the student who is correct. _____

   b   Explain why the other student is incorrect.

   _____

   _____

C1.3 Melting and freezing

A Fill in the gaps to complete the sentences.

The change of state from solid to liquid is called _____. When a solid warms up, its particles vibrate _____. The solid melts when its particles move _____ from their places in the pattern. A substance melts at its _____ point. A _____ substance has a sharp melting point. The change of state from a liquid to a solid is called _____. When a liquid cools, its particles move around more _____. It freezes when its particles get into a regular pattern and vibrate in fixed positions.

B Box **1** shows some particles in a liquid.

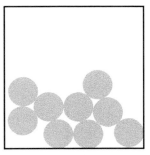

Box 1   Box 2

a Draw the same number of particles in box **2** to show how the particles might be arranged when the liquid in box **1** has frozen.

b Describe how the particle movement changes when a liquid freezes.

_____

_____

C Rashid has a hot liquid. He measures the temperature every minute as the liquid cools. His data are in the table.

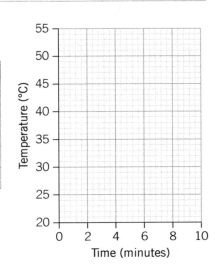

Time (min)	Temperature (°C)	Time (min)	Temperature (°C)
0	50	6	35
1	45	7	35
2	38	8	35
3	35	9	32
4	35	10	25
5	35		

Copy the axes on the right, and plot a graph to show the data in the table.
Then label the graph to show where the following statements are true.

• This is the melting point of the substance.

• The solid is cooling down.

• The particles are moving around more and more slowly.

• The particles are arranging themselves in a pattern.

• The particles are vibrating about fixed points.

• Some of the particles are moving around and some are vibrating about fixed points.

C1.4 Boiling

A Fill in the gaps to complete the sentences.

A substance can change from the liquid to the _____ state by boiling. Boiling happens when

bubbles of the substance in the _____ state form everywhere in the liquid and rise to the surface to

escape into the air. The total mass of the gas and _____ is the same as the mass of the liquid at the

start. Scientists say the mass is _____ in boiling. A substance boils at a certain temperature and this is

called its _____ point.

B The table gives some data for four substances.

Substance	Melting point (°C)	Boiling point (°C)
bromine	−7	59
mercury	−39	357
xenon	−112	−108

Complete the sentences below by writing the name of the substance being described. Use only the **boiling point** data to help you.

The substance with the lowest boiling point is _____. The substance with the strongest attractive forces

between particles in the liquid is _____. The substance that needs most energy to change an amount

containing 1 million particles from liquid to gas is _____.

C Draw a line to match each substance to its state at the given temperature. You will need to use **melting point data** and **boiling point data** from the table in activity **B**.

| bromine at 20 °C | | solid |
|------------------| |--------|
| mercury at 400 °C | | liquid |
| xenon at −115 °C | | gas |

D A student heats a liquid. The graph shows how its temperature changes with time.

The letters A, B, and C show different periods during the heating. Write **one**, **two**, or **three** letters next to each statement. You can use each letter once or more than once.

a In these periods, energy is transferred from the surroundings to the substance. _____

b In these periods, the particles move faster as temperature increases. _____

c In this period, the energy transferred is separating particles from each other to make bubbles of

gas. _____

d In this period, the energy transferred is making bubbles of gas escape from the liquid. _____

C1.5 More changes of state

A Fill in the gaps to complete the sentences.

A substance can change from the liquid to the _____ state by evaporation or boiling. Evaporation happens when particles leave the _____ of a liquid. The change of state from gas to liquid is called _____. The change of state from solid to gas is called _____.

B A student investigates how quickly drops of water evaporate in different places. He sets up the apparatus below.

The student puts each Petri dish in a different place: one on top of a heater, one in a fridge, and one on a windowsill. He measures the time taken for all the water to evaporate from each dish.

Complete the table with the names of the variables in the experiment.

Type of variable	Variable
independent	
dependent	
control	

C The statements below describe the arrangement and movement of particles in different states, and during changes of state.

1 The particles are arranged in a regular pattern. They vibrate on the spot.

2 The particles are spread out. They move around randomly.

3 The particles are arranged randomly, touching their neighbours. They move from place to place, sliding over each other.

4 More and more particles leave the liquid surface.

5 Some particles leave their place in the regular pattern. They move far away from their neighbours.

6 The particles move closer together.

7 Bubbles form everywhere in the liquid. In the bubbles, the particles are spread out.

8 Some particles, with more energy than the others, leave the liquid surface.

9 Bubbles rise to the surface and their particles leave the liquid.

Write down, **in the correct order**:

a The letters of three statements that explain what happens to particles during sublimation.

_____

b The letters of three statements that explain what happens to particles during condensation.

_____

c The letters of four statements that explain what happens to particles during evaporation.

_____

d The letters of four statements that explain what happens to particles during boiling.

_____

C1.6 Diffusion

A Fill in the gaps to complete the sentences.

The random movement and _____ of particles is called diffusion. Diffusion happens in the liquid

and _____ states because the particles in these states move around all the time. An example of

_____ is when a drop of ink spreads through water. The particles move by themselves. You do not

need to shake or _____.

B Edward puts some flowers in the corner of a room.

Half an hour later, he can smell the flowers wherever he is in the room.

Add some particles to the diagram to show why he can smell the flowers everywhere in the room.

a Draw each particle as a small circle.

b Explain why the particles you drew in part **a** have diffused.

_____

C A student investigates the diffusion of purple potassium manganate(VII) when it dissolves in water. She wants to find out how water temperature affects the time for the purple colour to spread out. She sets up the apparatus below.

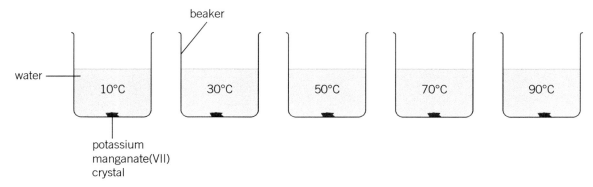

a Complete the table to identify the different types of variable in the investigation.

Variable	Type of variable
Time for the purple colour to spread out	
Size of crystals	
Temperature of water	
Volume of water	

b Explain why there will be uncertainty in the measurement of the dependent variable.

_____

c Explain why one of the control variables is not easy to control.

_____

d Predict what the results of the investigation will show.

_____

e Use particle theory to explain your prediction.

_____

C1.7 Gas pressure

A Fill in the gaps to complete the sentences.

The particles in a gas move randomly in _____ directions. When they move, they may hit – or

_____ with – the walls of the container. The collisions exert a _____ on the walls. The

force per unit area acting on a surface is the gas _____.

B Catherine is at the bottom of a mountain. She allows air to fill a glass jar (jar **X**) and screws on the lid. At the top of the mountain she allows air to fill another glass jar (jar **Y**). The diagrams show the particles in the jars.

Use particle theory to explain why the gas pressure in jar **Y** is less than the gas pressure in jar **X**, if both jars are at the same temperature.

Jar X   Jar Y

_____

_____

C Look at the diagrams in activity **B**. Tick the statements below to show whether they are true or false, or whether it is not possible to know.

Statement	✓ if it is definitely true	✓ if it is definitely false	✓ if it is not possible to know whether it is true or false
If the temperature in jar **X** increases, the pressure increases.			
If the temperature in jar **Y** increases, the pressure in jar **Y** will be greater than the pressure in jar **X**.			
If more particles are added to jar **Y**, the pressure will increase.			
If some particles are removed from jar **X**, the pressure in jar **X** will be less than the pressure in jar **Y**.			
If more particles are added to jar **X**, the pressure will decrease.			
If the temperature in jar **X** increases, the pressure in jar **X** will be greater than the pressure in jar **Y**.			

Pinchpoint question

Answer the question below, then do the follow-up activity **with the same letter** as the answer you picked.

The melting point of oxygen is −218 °C and its boiling point is −183 °C.

How are its particles arranged, and how do they move, at −200 °C?

A The particles are arranged randomly. They are close to their neighbours, but do not touch them. They move around randomly, sliding over each other.

B The particles are arranged randomly. They are far apart from each other. They move around randomly, throughout the container.

C The particles are arranged randomly. They touch their neighbours. They move around randomly, sliding over each other.

D The particles are arranged in a pattern. They are far apart from each other. They vibrate on the spot.

Follow-up activities

A Keira draws some particles in liquid water.

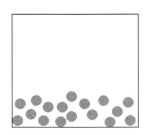

    a   **i**   Write down **two** things that she has drawn correctly in her drawing.

        1 _____

        2 _____

       ii   Write down **one** thing that she has drawn incorrectly. _____

    b   In the box, draw the correct arrangement of particles in liquid water.

Hint: How close together are the particles in a liquid? For help see C1 1.2 States of matter.

B Complete the table to give the state of each substance at **−100 °C**.

Substance	Melting point (°C)	Boiling point (°C)	State at −100 °C
argon	−189	−186	
chlorine	−101	−35	
mercury	−39	357	
xenon	−112	−108	
ytterbium	824	1430	
zirconium	1850	3580	

Hint: Sketch a temperature scale for the first substance, and label the melting point and boiling point. Then use the scale to work out the state of this substance at −100 °C. Repeat for the other substances. For help, see C1 1.4 Boiling.

C The melting point of bromine is −7 °C and its boiling point is 59 °C.

Draw a line to match each temperature to the correct description of the arrangement and to the correct description of movement of bromine particles at that temperature.

Temperature (°C)	Particle arrangement	Particle movement
58		
	regular pattern	random, throughout the container
−5		
	random and touching	random, sliding over each other
60		
	random and far apart	vibrating on the spot
−10		

Hint: Start by using the melting and boiling point data to work out the state of bromine at each temperature. Then draw a line to match each state to the correct description of the particle arrangement and movement. For help see C1 1.2 States of matter, C1 1.3 Melting and freezing, and C1 1.4 Boiling.

D a Draw one diagram in each box below to show particles of a substance in the solid, liquid, and gas states.

solid	liquid	gas

b Complete the sentences below to describe how the particles are moving in each state.

In the solid state, the particles

_____

In the liquid state, the particles

_____

In the gas state, the particles

_____

Hint: Do not confuse the particle movement and arrangement in different states. For help, see C1 1.2 States of matter.

Pinchpoint review

Now look back at the question – do you think you chose the right letter?
Turn to the Answers page to find out.

C2.1 Elements

A Fill in the gaps to complete the sentences.

An element is a substance that _____ be broken down into other substances. There are about

100 elements, which are grouped and listed in the _____ Table. Every element has its own

_____ symbol, which is a one- or two-letter code for the element. Scientists all over the world use

the same chemical _____ for the elements.

B Write down definitions of:

a an element

_____

b a chemical symbol

_____

C Complete the table by writing down the name or chemical symbol of each element.

Name of element	Chemical symbol
hydrogen	
	He
zinc	
	W
iron	
	Au

Hint: Use a Periodic table to help you.

D The table gives the properties of some elements.

Use information from the table to answer the questions below.

Element	State at 20 °C	Appearance	Mass of 1 cm³ (g)	Other properties
aluminium	solid	shiny silver-coloured	2.70	Good conductor of electricity. Not damaged by air or water.
argon	gas	colourless	0.0016	Does not join to, or damage, other substances.
arsenic	solid	shiny grey	5.72	Toxic to insects, bacteria and mammals.
gold	solid	shiny yellow	19.3	Good conductor of electricity. Not damaged by air or water.

a Explain why gold is used to make connectors in electronic devices.

_____

b Explain why many aeroplanes are made from aluminium, not gold.

_____

c Explain why some important documents are stored in argon.

_____

d In the past, arsenic-containing substances were used to prevent insects damaging apple trees. Suggest why they are no longer used for this purpose.

_____

A Fill in the gaps to complete the sentences.

Elements are made up of _____ . An atom is the _____ part of an element that can

exist. All the _____ of an element are the same. The atoms of one element are _____

from the atoms of all the other elements. The properties of an element are the properties of _____

atoms joined together.

B The table shows data about the atoms of three elements.

Element	Radius of atom (nm)	Relative mass of atom
copper	0.128	64
mercury	0.152	201
zinc	0.133	65

Hint: The radius of an atom shows its size. The greater the radius, the bigger the atom. In your answer, you could use phrases such as 'greater than' or 'bigger than'.

Write down three sentences to compare the data for the three elements.

_____

_____

_____

C The statements below are about two elements, copper and zinc.

a Tick the statements that are true.

    1 An element is the smallest part of an atom that can exist. ☐

    2 The atoms of copper are all the same as each other. ☐

    3 The atoms of copper are the same as the atoms of zinc. ☐

    4 A single atom of zinc has the same properties as a piece of zinc wire. ☐

    5 A copper wire can conduct electricity, but a single copper atom cannot conduct electricity. ☐

b Now write corrected versions of the **three** statements above that are not true.

_____

_____

_____

D A piece of solid copper melts.

a Describe the changes in the arrangement and movement of its atoms.

_____

_____

b Explain why one copper atom on its own cannot melt.

_____

_____

C2.3 Compounds

A Fill in the gaps to complete the sentences.

A compound is a substance that is made up of atoms of _____ or more elements. The atoms are

_____ joined together. The properties of a compound are _____ from the properties

of the elements whose atoms are in it because the atoms are joined together to make _____

substance. A _____ is a group of atoms that are joined together strongly.

B The diagrams show molecules of elements and compounds.

key
- oxygen atom
- nitrogen atom
- hydrogen atom

dinitrogen monoxide

    a Draw circles around the molecules of compounds.

    b Explain why the diagrams you circled are compounds.

    _____

C Nitrogen and oxygen are gases in the air. They are elements.
Oxygen helps substances to burn. Crisp bags are filled with nitrogen to stop the crisps going stale.
Dinitrogen monoxide is a compound. It is used to relieve pain in childbirth.

Choose molecule diagrams from activity **B** to help you to answer the questions below.

    a Write down the number of atoms in one nitrogen molecule. _____

    b Write down the number of atoms in one dinitrogen monoxide molecule. _____

    c Write down the number of elements whose atoms are in one nitrogen molecule. _____

    d Write down the number of elements whose atoms are in one dinitrogen monoxide molecule. _____

D The table shows the properties of three substances.

Substance	Melting point (°C)	Appearance	Is it attracted to a magnet?
iron	1535	shiny and grey	yes
sulfur	113	yellow	no
iron sulfide	1194	shiny and grey	no

    a Describe **one** way in which iron sulfide is similar to the elements it is made from.

    _____

    b Describe **two** ways in which iron sulfide is different from the elements it is made from.

    _____

    c Suggest why most of the properties of iron sulfide are different from the properties of the elements it is
made from.

    _____

C2.4 Chemical formulae

A Fill in the gaps to complete the sentences.

A _____ formula uses chemical symbols to show the elements in a substance. It also shows the

number of atoms of one element compared to the _____ of atoms of another element. For example,

the chemical formula of water is H_2O. This shows that water is made up of two elements – hydrogen and

_____. It also shows that there are two atoms of hydrogen for every _____ atom of oxygen.

B Complete the table.

Name of compound	Atoms in compound	Formula of compound
magnesium oxide	one atom of magnesium for every one atom of oxygen	
calcium chloride		$CaCl_2$
	one atom of nitrogen for every two atoms of oxygen	NO_2
carbon monoxide		
sulfur trioxide		

C Complete the sentences below by writing one **number** in each gap.

Sulfur dioxide, SO_2, has _____ oxygen atoms for every one sulfur atom. The total number of atoms in one sulfur

dioxide molecule is _____.

Methane, CH_4, is a gas used for cooking. It has _____ hydrogen atoms for every one carbon atom. The total number

of atoms in one methane molecule is _____.

Ethanol, C_2H_6O, is the compound in alcoholic drinks. Its molecules have atoms of _____ different elements. It has

_____ hydrogen atoms for every one carbon atom.

D Ibuprofen is a painkiller. It exists as molecules. Its formula is $C_{13}H_{18}O_2$.
Write three sentences to explain what the formula of ibuprofen shows.

_____

_____

_____

E The table shows the relative masses of atoms of three elements.

Element	Relative mass of atoms
hydrogen	1
carbon	12
oxygen	16

Calculate the relative formula mass of the elements and compounds below. Show your working.

a Oxygen, O_2

_____

b Water, H_2O

_____

c Ibuprofen, $C_{13}H_{18}O_2$

_____

C1 Chapter 2 Pinchpoint

Pinchpoint question

Answer the question below, then do the follow-up activity **with the same letter** as the answer you picked.

Paracetamol is a painkiller. A molecule of paracetamol is made up of 8 carbon atoms, 9 hydrogen atoms, 1 nitrogen atom, and 2 oxygen atoms.

What is its chemical formula?

A CHNO

B $_8C_9H_1N_2O$

C $C_8H_9NO_2$

D $Ca_8H_9NiO_2$

Follow-up activities

A Complete the table below by writing the chemical formula of each substance.

Substance	Relative number of atoms of each element in the substance	Chemical formula
carbon dioxide	1 atom of carbon 2 atoms of oxygen	
propane, used in camping stoves	3 atoms of carbon 8 atoms of hydrogen	
ethanoic acid, an ingredient of vinegar	2 atoms of carbon 4 atoms of hydrogen 2 atoms of oxygen	
aspirin, used to help prevent heart attacks	9 atoms of carbon 8 atoms of hydrogen 4 atoms of oxygen	
lidocaine, a local anaesthetic	14 atoms of carbon 22 atoms of hydrogen 2 atoms of nitrogen 1 atom of oxygen	

Hint: The small number on the right of each chemical symbol in a formula gives the relative number of atoms of that element in the formula. For help, see C1 2.4 Chemical formulae.

B Write down the chemical formulae of the substances below.

Nitrogen gas, with molecules made up of two nitrogen atoms. _____

Water, with two atoms of hydrogen for every one atom of oxygen. _____

Sulfur trioxide, with one atom of sulfur for every three atoms of oxygen. _____

Dinitrogen tetroxide, with two atoms of nitrogen for four atoms of oxygen. _____

Hint: Write small numbers on the right of each chemical symbol to show the relative number of atoms of this element that are in the formula. For help, see C1 2.4 Chemical formulae.

C Draw a line to match each molecule diagram to its chemical formula.

Key

 oxygen atom carbon atom ○ hydrogen atom

CH$_4$		
H$_2$O		
C$_2$H$_5$OH		
CH$_3$COOH		
C$_3$H$_8$		

Hint: Start by counting the number of atoms of each element shown in each diagram. For help, see C1 2.4 Chemical formulae.

D Complete the table by writing the chemical symbol of each element next to its name.

Name of element	Chemical symbol
calcium	
carbon	
chlorine	
nickel	

Name of element	Chemical symbol
nitrogen	
hydrogen	
oxygen	
sodium	

Hint: The chemical symbols are listed in the Periodic table. Make sure you write the first letter upper case, and the second letter lower case. For example, the formula of magnesium is Mg, not MG or mg or mG. For help, see C1 2.1 Elements.

 Pinchpoint review

Now look back at the question – do you think you chose the right letter?
Turn to the Answers page to find out.

C3.1 Chemical reactions

A Fill in the gaps to complete the sentences.

A chemical reaction is a change that makes _____ substances. In a chemical reaction, the atoms in the starting substances are _____ and join together _____. It is _____ easy to reverse a chemical reaction. Chemical reactions involve _____ transfers to or from the surroundings. Chemists use _____ to speed up reactions. Not all changes involve chemical reactions. A _____ change, such as melting, is usually reversible.

B The diagrams below show the atoms in some physical changes and chemical reactions.

a Write down the letters of the diagrams that show chemical reactions. _____

b Explain how you decided which diagrams show chemical reactions.

_____

C Tick to show whether each statement is true for chemical reactions, physical changes, or both.

Statement	✓ if true for chemical reactions	✓ if true for physical changes
In this type of change, new substances are made.		
This type of change is easily reversible.		
This type of change involves energy transfers.		
In this type of change the atoms are rearranged and join together differently.		

D a Write a paragraph to compare physical changes with chemical reactions.

_____

_____

_____

_____

_____

_____

b Use ideas about atoms to explain the differences you have described.

_____

_____

_____

C3.2 Word equations

A Fill in the gaps to complete the sentences.

The starting substances in a chemical reaction are called _____. The substances that are made

in a chemical reaction are called _____. In a word equation, the reactants are on the

_____ of the arrow and the products are on the _____ of the arrow. The

_____ means 'reacts to make'.

B Heptane is one of the substances in petrol. The word equation shows its burning reaction.

heptane + oxygen → carbon dioxide + water

In the word equation, circle each **reactant in pencil** and each **product in pen**.

C Write a word equation for each reaction below.

a Calcium burns in oxygen to make calcium oxide.

_____

b Sodium reacts with chlorine to make sodium chloride.

_____

c Iron reacts with chlorine to make iron chloride.

_____

d Methane burns in oxygen to make carbon dioxide and water.

_____

D Balance the equations below.
Make sure there are the same number of atoms of each element on both sides of the arrow.

a ___ $Mg + O_2 \rightarrow$ ___ MgO

b ___ $Na + Br_2 \rightarrow$ ___ $NaBr$

c ___ $Fe +$ ___ $Cl_2 \rightarrow$ ___ $FeCl_3$

d ___ $C_3H_8 +$ ___ $O_2 \rightarrow$ ___$CO_2 +$ ___ H_2O

Hint: Do not change the little numbers in the formulae.

E Write balanced symbol equations for the reactions in activity **C**.
Use only the formulae in the table.

a _____

b _____

c _____

d _____

Substance	Formula
calcium	Ca
oxygen	O_2
sodium	Na
chlorine	Cl_2
iron	Fe

Substance	Formula
carbon dioxide	CO_2
water	H_2O
calcium oxide	CaO
sodium chloride	NaCl
iron chloride	$FeCl_3$
methane	CH_4

C3.3 Burning fuels

A Fill in the gaps to complete the sentences.

A fuel is a material that burns to transfer _____ by heating. The scientific word for burning is

_____ . When a fuel burns it reacts with _____ from the air. The product of combustion

of carbon is _____ _____ . The products of combustion of a compound that is made

from carbon and hydrogen atoms are carbon dioxide and _____ . Burning reactions are oxidation

reactions. In oxidation reactions, substances react with _____ .

B The products of a combustion reaction are the substances that are made when a substance burns.
Complete the table with the names of the products of combustion.
Then complete the balanced symbol equations by writing in the missing formulae and balancing numbers.

Fuel	Product or products of combustion	Equation for combustion reaction
carbon		$C + O_2 \rightarrow$ _____
hydrogen		$2H_2 + O_2 \rightarrow 2$ _____
heptane (a compound of carbon and hydrogen that is in petrol)		$C_7H_{16} +$ __$O_2 \rightarrow 7$_____ $+$ __H_2O

C Riley does an investigation to compare the increase in temperature of water when two different fuels burn. Here is a diagram of the apparatus. The fuels are wax and ethanol.

clamp — test tube
water — water
wax — ethanol

a Draw a line to match each variable to the type of variable it is in this investigation.

volume of water

increase in temperature of water

fuel

distance of flame from test tube

independent

dependent

control

b Suggest one improvement that Riley could make to maximise the amount of energy transferred from the fuel to the water.

_____

_____

c Explain why it is important for Riley to know the mass of each fuel burnt in the investigation.

_____

_____

C3.4 Thermal decomposition

A Fill in the gaps to complete the sentences.

In a decomposition reaction, _____ reactant breaks down to make _____ or more

products. The reactant must be a _____. The products can be elements or _____.

Zinc carbonate, for example, decomposes to make zinc _____ and _____

_____. When heat is needed to make a substance break down, the reaction is called a

_____ decomposition reaction.

B Highlight or underline the **two** word equations that show decomposition reactions.

W calcium carbonate → calcium oxide + carbon dioxide
X magnesium + nitrogen → magnesium nitride
Y methane + oxygen → carbon dioxide + water
Z sodium nitrate → sodium nitrite + oxygen

C The word equations below show four thermal decomposition reactions:

copper carbonate → copper oxide + carbon dioxide

zinc carbonate → zinc oxide + carbon dioxide

calcium nitrate → calcium oxide + nitrogen dioxide + oxygen

magnesium nitrate → magnesium oxide + nitrogen dioxide + oxygen

a Predict the names of the products of the thermal decomposition reaction of lead carbonate.

_____

b Predict the names of the products of the thermal decomposition reaction of strontium nitrate.

_____

D Raj heats copper carbonate in the apparatus shown in the diagram.

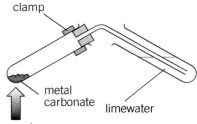

He writes the time for the limewater to go milky in the table below.

He then repeats the experiment with two more compounds.

Compound	Time for limewater to start looking cloudy (minutes)
copper carbonate	1
potassium carbonate	did not go cloudy after heating for 10 minutes
lead carbonate	4

Write a conclusion for Raj's investigation.
In your conclusion, name which carbonate decomposes most easily.

_____

_____

_____

C3.5 Conservation of mass

A Fill in the gaps to complete the sentences.

In a chemical reaction or in a _____ change, the total mass does not change. This means that in a

chemical reaction, the total mass of reactants is equal to the total mass of _____. This is the law of

_____ of mass. Balanced symbol equations show the relative amounts of _____ and

products.

B Hydrogen and oxygen react together to make water:

hydrogen + oxygen → water

The diagrams show some of the atoms before and after the reaction.

Before the reaction   After the reaction

Use the diagrams to explain why the total mass of hydrogen and oxygen that reacts is the same as the mass of
water made.

_____

C Calculate the missing masses in the reactions below.

a   carbon   +   oxygen   →   carbon dioxide
              12 g   32 g   _____ g

b   calcium carbonate   →   calcium oxide   +   carbon dioxide
              10 g   5.6 g   _____ g

c   calcium nitrate   →   calcium oxide   +   nitrogen dioxide   +   oxygen
              32.8 g   _____ g   18.4 g   3.2 g

D A teacher demonstrates three reactions.

Tick one column next to each reaction to show whether the mass of the substances in the reaction vessel increases,
decreases, or does not change.

	Reaction	✓ if mass increases	✓ if mass decreases	✓ if mass does not change
a	Solid lead nitrate reacts with solid potassium iodide to make solid lead iodide and solid potassium nitrate			
b	Solid magnesium reacts with oxygen gas from the air to make solid magnesium oxide.			
c	Solid copper carbonate decomposes to make solid copper oxide and carbon dioxide gas.			
d	aluminium (solid) + iodine (solid) → aluminium iodide (solid)			

e Explain your answers to parts **b** and **d**.

_____

_____

_____

C3.6 Exothermic and endothermic

A Fill in the gaps to complete the sentences.

Chemical reactions involve _____ transfers.

Exothermic reactions transfer energy _____ the reaction mixture _____ the surroundings.

This causes the temperature of the surroundings to _____ .

Endothermic reactions transfer energy _____ the surroundings _____ the reaction

mixture. This causes the temperature of the surroundings to _____ .

B Barney sets up the apparatus below.

He pours dilute hydrochloric acid into the cup, and measures its
temperature.

Then he adds a piece of magnesium ribbon. There is a chemical
reaction.

At the end of the chemical reaction he measures the temperature
again.

Then Barney repeats the experiment with zinc instead of magnesium.

Some of his results are in the table.

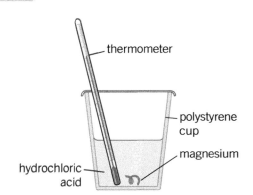

Reacting substances	Temperature before the reaction (°C)	Temperature after the reaction (°C)
hydrochloric acid and magnesium	20	28
hydrochloric acid and zinc	20	25

Write a conclusion for Barney's experiment.

_____

_____

_____

_____

C Sarah investigates the temperature changes
when different substances dissolve in water.
First, she uses a data book to find out whether
each substance dissolves exothermically or
endothermically.

Substance	Does it dissolve exothermically or endothermically?
aluminium chloride	exothermically
sodium chloride	endothermically
magnesium chloride	exothermically
potassium chloride	endothermically

a Predict the two substances in the table that make the temperature of the water increase at first when they
dissolve in water.

_____ and _____

b Aluminium chloride transfers more heat to the surroundings when it dissolves than magnesium chloride does.
Predict whether magnesium chloride or aluminium chloride results in the greater temperature change when it
dissolves in water.

_____

Pinchpoint question

Answer the question below, then do the follow-up activity **with the same letter** as the answer you picked.

A student heats copper carbonate in test tube **X**.

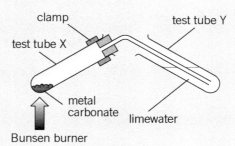

The copper carbonate decomposes to make copper oxide and carbon dioxide gas:

copper carbonate	→	copper oxide	+	carbon dioxide
(solid)		(solid)		(gas)

The gas bubbles into the limewater in test tube **Y**. Another chemical reaction takes place. The products are in the solid and liquid states.

Which statement correctly describes and explains any changes in mass in the contents of test tubes **X** and **Y**?

A The mass of **X** does not change because the product that leaves **X** is in the gas state.
   The mass of **Y** does not change because the reactant that enters **Y** is in the gas state.

B The masses of **X** and **Y** do not change because, for the chemical reaction in each test tube, the total mass of products is equal to total mass of reactants.

C The masses of **X** and **Y** increase because new substances are made in each test tube.

D The mass of **X** decreases because a product in the gas state leaves the test tube.
   The mass of **Y** increases because a reactant in the gas state enters the test tube.

Follow-up activities

A The diagrams show particles when a substance is in the solid state and when it is in the gas state.

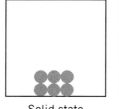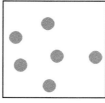

Solid state   Gas state

Tick the statements below that are true.

1 A particle has the same mass when the substance is in the solid and gas states. ☐

2 One thousand particles of a substance in the gas state have a smaller mass than one thousand particles of the same substance in the solid state. ☐

3 A particle has no mass when the substance is in the gas state. ☐

4 A gas has mass. ☐

Hint: Do the particles change when a substance changes state? For help, see C1 1.2 States of matter.

B A teacher demonstrates three reactions.
Draw a line to show, for each reaction, whether the total mass of solid substance(s) in the reaction vessel increases, decreases, or does not change. You can choose an option more than once.

Solid calcium carbonate decomposes to make solid calcium oxide and carbon dioxide gas.	mass increases
Solid carbon reacts with oxygen from the air to make carbon dioxide gas.	mass decreases
Solid magnesium reacts with oxygen from the air to make solid magnesium oxide.	mass does not change

Hint: How does the mass change if the reaction makes a gas, which escapes to the air? For help, see C1 3.5 Conservation of mass.

C The diagrams show some atoms before and after the chemical reaction of nitrogen and oxygen to make nitrogen monoxide.

Each sentence below has one mistake. Write a corrected version of each sentence.

Reactants   Product

a In the chemical reaction, the atoms are not rearranged.

_____

b In the chemical reaction, the atoms are joined together in the same way before and after the reaction.

_____

c There are more atoms in the products than in the reactants.

_____

d The total mass of products is greater than the total mass of reactants.

_____

Hint: Are new atoms made in chemical reactions? For help, see C1 3.2 Word equations and C1 3.5 Conservation of mass.

D Explain each observation below.

a On burning solid magnesium in air, the mass of solid product is greater than the mass of solid reactant.

_____

_____

b On heating lead carbonate to make it decompose, the mass of solid product is less than the mass of solid reactant.

_____

_____

Hint: What are the states of the reactants and products in each reaction? For help see C1 3.5 Conservation of mass.

⊗ **Pinchpoint review**

Now look back at the question – do you think you chose the right letter?
Turn to the Answers page to find out.

C4.1 Acids and alkalis

A Fill in the gaps to complete the sentences.

Do **not** taste or feel substances in science unless your teacher tells you to. Acids taste _____ and

alkalis feel _____. Wear safety glasses or safety goggles when working with acids and alkalis because

many of these substances are _____. This means that they burn eyes and _____. A

concentrated solution of alkali has more alkali particles in it than a _____ solution.

B This hazard symbol is displayed on bottles that contain some acids and alkalis.

Complete the table below.

Risk from this hazard	How to control this risk
damaging your eyes	
	wear plastic gloves

C Ms Khan has two bottles of sulfuric acid, **X** and **Y**. There is one litre of acid in each bottle.

- The acid in bottle **X** is concentrated.
- The acid in bottle **Y** is dilute.

a Predict one difference in the properties of the acids in bottles **X** and **Y**.

_____

b Give a reason for the difference you predicted in your answer to part **a**.
In your answer, compare the numbers of acid particles in the two bottles.

_____

c Suggest how Ms Khan could make the acid in bottle **X** more dilute.

_____

D Acidic solutions include H^+ particles and alkaline solutions include OH^- particles.

a Describe **one** way in which the particles in acids and alkalis are similar.

_____

_____

b Describe **two** ways in which the particles in acids and alkalis are different.

_____

_____

_____

_____

C4.2 Indicators and pH

A Fill in the gaps to complete the sentences.

Indicators show whether a solution is acidic, alkaline, or _____. Universal indicator is

_____ or orange or yellow in acids, green in _____ solutions, and blue or purple in

_____ solutions. The _____ scale measures how acidic or alkaline a solution is. The

pH of an acid is _____ than 7. The pH of a _____ solution is 7. The pH of an alkali is

_____ than 7.

B The table shows the colours of four indicators in dilute acids and alkalis.

Indicator	Colour in dilute hydrochloric acid	Colour in dilute sodium hydroxide solution (an alkali)
red cabbage	red	yellow or green
litmus	red	blue
methyl orange	red	yellow
phenolphthalein	colourless	pink

Ben adds a few drops of different indicators to some different solutions.
Draw a line to match each observation to a conclusion. You can choose an option more than once.

Observation

A colourless solution becomes yellow when a few drops of methyl orange are added.

A colourless solution remains colourless when a few drops of phenolphthalein are added.

A colourless solution becomes yellow when a few drops of red cabbage indicator are added.

Conclusion

The solution is neutral.

The solution is acidic.

The solution is alkaline.

C a Explain why there is uncertainty in pH values that are measured using universal indicator.

_____

b Describe a method of measuring pH that gives more accurate values than universal indicator.

_____

D The table gives the pH values of six solutions.

a List the letters of the solutions in order of increasing acidity (most alkaline solution first).

_____

b Give the letters of three solutions that could be ethanoic acid.

_____

Solution	pH
U	7.1
V	3.2
W	9.5
X	13.8
Y	2.4
Z	3.7

c Give the letter of the ethanoic acid solution that is most concentrated. _____
Explain your decision.

_____

C4.3 Neutralisation

A Fill in the gaps to complete the sentences.

When a base reacts with an acid the acid is _____ by the base. If you add a base to an acid the pH

_____ . If you add an acid to a base, the pH _____ .

B The soil on Frank's farm is acidic. He adds a base to the soil.

    a Describe what happens to the pH of the soil when Frank adds the base.

    _____

    b Suggest why Frank wants to change the pH of the soil.

    _____

    _____

    c Give one example of another useful neutralisation reaction.

    _____

C Ash investigates three different types of indigestion tablets.
He measures the volume of acid that each tablet can neutralise.

Complete the table to show the different types of variable in Ash's investigation.

Type of variable	Variable
Independent	
Dependent	
Control	
Control	
Control	

D Samira adds an alkaline solution, 1 cm³ at a time, to an acid.

She uses a pH probe and data logger to measure the pH. The graph shows her results.

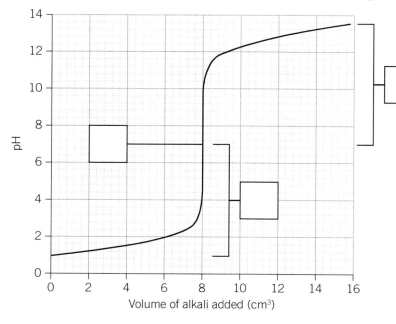

In each box, write the letters of **one or two** of the statements below.

V	The mixture is acidic.
W	All the acid has been neutralised.
X	The alkali is neutralising the acid.
Y	The mixture is neutral.
Z	The mixture is alkaline.

C4.4 Making salts

A Fill in the gaps to complete the sentences.

When an acid reacts with a metal or a base, one of the products is a _____. Hydrochloric acid makes

_____ salts. Sulfuric acid makes _____ salts. When an acid reacts to make a salt, metal

atoms replace the _____ atoms that were in the acid.

B The statements below can be reordered to describe how to make a salt from zinc oxide and hydrochloric acid. Read the statements and write down the order of statements that you think will give the best description.

Best order ☐ ☐ ☐ ☐ ☐ ☐ ☐

1 Filter to remove unreacted zinc oxide.

2 Stop adding zinc oxide when some zinc oxide is left over.

3 Leave the evaporating dish and its contents in a warm, dry place.

4 Pour some dilute hydrochloric acid into a beaker.

5 Heat the zinc chloride solution in an evaporating basin.

6 Add zinc oxide powder to the acid, one spatula at a time, while stirring.

7 Stop heating when about half the water has evaporated.

C Complete the table by adding the names of the salts formed in each reaction.

	Reactants	Name of salt formed	Name of other product formed
a	magnesium and sulfuric acid		hydrogen
b	zinc and hydrochloric acid		hydrogen
c	copper oxide and hydrochloric acid		water
d	sodium hydroxide and sulfuric acid		water
e	potassium hydroxide and hydrochloric acid		water

D Write word equations for the reactions in the table in activity **C**.

a _____

b _____

c _____

d _____

e _____

E The word equations below show some reactions that form salts. Write a balanced symbol equation under each word equation. Use the formulae in the table.

a zinc + sulfuric acid → zinc sulfate + hydrogen

_____

b magnesium + hydrochloric acid → magnesium chloride + hydrogen

_____

c copper oxide + sulfuric acid → copper sulfate + water

_____

d sodium hydroxide + hydrochloric acid → sodium chloride + water

_____

Substance	Formula
zinc	Zn
magnesium	Mg
copper oxide	CuO
sodium hydroxide	$NaOH$
sulfuric acid	H_2SO_4
hydrochloric acid	HCl
zinc sulfate	$ZnSO_4$
magnesium chloride	$MgCl_2$
copper sulfate	$CuSO_4$
hydrogen	H_2
water	H_2O
sodium chloride	$NaCl$

Pinchpoint question

Answer the question below, then do the follow-up activity **with the same letter** as the answer you picked.

Lyra has some acid. Its pH is 3. She adds water and measures the pH. Then she adds sodium hydroxide solution and measures the pH again.
Which set of results could be correct?

	pH at start	pH after adding water	pH after adding sodium hydroxide solution
A	3	8	1
B	3	2	1
C	3	4	5
D	3	2	5

Follow-up activities

A Each sentence below has one mistake. Write a corrected version of each sentence.

a   Adding water to an acid makes the solution less dilute.

_____

b   When an acid is diluted, it has more acid particles per litre.

_____

c   The greater the number of acid particles per litre, the higher the pH.

_____

d   Adding alkali to an acid dilutes some or all of the acid.

_____

e   Neutralising an acid decreases the pH of the solution.

_____

Hint: What happens to pH as a solution gets less acidic? For help see C1 4.1 Acids and alkalis, C1 4.2 Indicators and pH, and C1 4.3 Neutralisation.

B In each question below, circle the correct pH.

a   The most acidic solution   1   4   6
b   The most alkaline solution   8   11   14
c   The least acidic solution   2   3   5
d   The least alkaline solution   9   12   13
e   The neutral solution   6   7   8

Hint: What is the pH range of acidic solutions? For help see C1 4.2 Indicators and pH.

C Draw a line to match each action to the correct observation and explanation.

Action	Observation	Explanation
Adding water to an alkaline solution	pH increases, but not above 7.	Some of the alkali has been neutralised so there are fewer particles of alkali per litre.
Adding acid to an alkaline solution	pH increases, possibly above 7.	The solution has been diluted so there are fewer particles of acid per litre.
Adding water to an acidic solution	pH decreases, but not below 7.	Some of the acid has been neutralised so there are fewer particles of acid per litre.
Adding alkali to an acidic solution	pH decreases, possibly below 7.	The solution has been diluted so there are fewer particles of alkali per litre.

Hint: Can an acidic solution become alkaline when water alone is added to it? For help see C1 4.1 Acids and alkalis, C1 4.2 Indicators and pH, and C1 4.3 Neutralisation.

D The diagrams show two acid solutions.

One solution is more concentrated than the other.

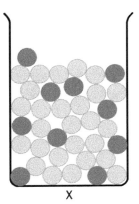
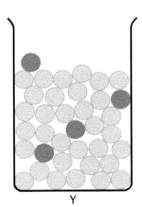

Key
● Acid particle   ○ Water particle

X   Y

Tick the statements below that are true.

1 Solution X has more acid particles per litre than solution Y. ☐

2 Solution X is less concentrated than solution Y. ☐

3 Solution Y is more dilute than solution X. ☐

4 Adding more water to solution X would concentrate the solution. ☐

5 Adding more water to solution Y would dilute the solution. ☐

Hint: Does a more concentrated acid have more or fewer acid particles per litre? For help see C1 4.1 Acids and alkalis.

 Pinchpoint review

Now look back at the question – do you think you chose the right letter?

Turn to the Answers page to find out.

C1 Revision questions

1 ⚗⚗ Gallium arsenide is a compound that is used in electronic devices. It is also used in some solar cells.

  a Define the term 'compound'. *(1 mark)*

_____

  b The formula of gallium arsenide is GaAs. Use the Periodic table at the back of the book to name the two elements whose atoms are in the compound. *(1 mark)*

_____ and _____

  c Gallium arsenide is made in a chemical reaction of the two elements you named in part **b**. Write a word equation for the reaction. *(1 mark)*

_____

2 ⚗⚗ Caffeine is a substance that is in tea, coffee, and chocolate. It makes people feel more alert, and quickens the heart rate.
The chemical formula of caffeine is $C_8H_{10}N_4O_2$.

  a Write how many different **types** of atom are in a caffeine molecule. *(1 mark)*

_____

  b Calculate the total number of atoms in a caffeine molecule. Show your working. *(2 marks)*

_____

  c A mixture of caffeine and water has a pH of 6.9. Determine whether the mixture is acidic, alkaline, or neutral. *(1 mark)*

_____

  d The melting point of caffeine is 237 °C. Describe the arrangement and movement of caffeine molecules at room temperature, 20 °C. *(2 marks)*

_____

_____

_____

_____

  e A scientist has some solid caffeine. She heats it up. Describe how the arrangement and movement of the caffeine molecules change at 237 °C. *(2 marks)*

_____

_____

_____

3 ⚗⚗ Fingerprints help to solve crimes, but fingerprints on plastic are often invisible. Forensic scientists can use gold to make fingerprints visible. They place a tiny amount of solid gold in a container with the piece of plastic. They take the air out of the container, and make the gold sublime. A thin film of solid gold deposits on the plastic, and the fingerprints become visible.

  a Gold is an element. Define the term 'element'. *(1 mark)*

_____

  b Give the chemical symbol of gold. *(1 mark)*

_____

  c Use the particle model to explain subliming. *(2 marks)*

_____

_____

_____

  d Explain why subliming is a physical change, not a chemical reaction. *(2 marks)*

_____

_____

_____

_____

_____

4 ⚗⚗ Lithium nitrate decomposes on heating. The word equation shows the reaction.

lithium nitrate → lithium oxide + nitrogen dioxide
+ oxygen

  a Explain how the word equation shows that the reaction is a decomposition reaction. *(1 mark)*

_____

_____

b A teacher wanted to demonstrate the decomposition reaction of lithium nitrate at school. He looked up the hazard symbols for nitrogen dioxide gas. Two of these are shown in **Figure 1**.

Figure 1

Use the hazard symbols to suggest why the teacher decided not to do the demonstration.

(2 marks)

_____

_____

_____

_____

c A university student took suitable safety precautions. She placed 2.76 g of lithium nitrate in an open test tube and heated strongly. When the chemical reaction finished, the mass of solid lithium oxide in the test tube was 0.60 g.

i Use the particle model to explain why the nitrogen dioxide gas and oxygen gas that were made in the reaction escaped from the test tube.

(2 marks)

_____

_____

_____

_____

ii Calculate the total mass of nitrogen dioxide gas and oxygen gas that were made in the reaction. Show your working. *(2 marks)*

_____

d Balance the formula equation for the decomposition reaction by writing one number on each answer line.

$4LiNO_3 \rightarrow$ ____$Li_2O +$ ____$NO_2 + O_2$ *(1 mark)*

5 ⚠⚠ Doctors give zinc sulfate tablets to people with big skin burns. A student makes zinc sulfate crystals from zinc oxide and an acid. This is the method used.

Step 1   Add zinc oxide to dilute acid. Stop adding when some zinc oxide is left over.

Step 2   Filter the mixture.

Step 3   Pour the zinc sulfate solution into an evaporating dish.

Step 4   Heat until all the water has evaporated.

a Name the acid the student needs in step 1.

(1 mark)

_____

b What type of reaction is the reaction in step 1? Tick **one** box. *(1 mark)*

combustion ☐   neutralisation ☐

decomposition ☐   physical ☐

c Write a word equation for the reaction in step 1. *(1 mark)*

_____

d Write a formula equation for the reaction in step 1. Use the formulae in **Table 1**. *(2 marks)*

_____

Table 1

Substance	Formula
zinc oxide	ZnO
sulfuric acid	H_2SO_4
zinc sulfate	$ZnSO_4$
water	H_2O

e Name the substance left in the filter paper in step 2. *(1 mark)*

_____

f Suggest one improvement to step 4 to make the crystals as big as possible. *(1 mark)*

_____

g Write down two safety precautions the student should take in step 4. *(2 marks)*

_____

_____

6 🔬🔬 Some students investigate indigestion tablets. They measure the volume of acid that each tablet can neutralise. Their results are in **Table 2**.

Table 2

Type of tablet	Volume of acid that the tablet can neutralise (cm³)			
	first measure-ment	second measure-ment	third measure-ment	mean
X	10	9	10	
Y	2	2	2	
Z	5	11	5	

a Name the type of substance that must be present in all three tablets, in order to neutralise the acid.
(1 mark)

b Circle the outlier in **Table 2**. *(1 mark)*

c Calculate the mean volume of acid needed to neutralise tablet **X**. Show your working.
(2 marks)

d The students decide to plot their results on a line graph. Explain why it is better to draw a bar chart, not a line graph. *(1 mark)*

e Write a conclusion for the investigation. *(1 mark)*

7 🔬🔬 Sam works at a swimming pool. The pH of the water should be 7.4. Sam checks the water pH every day. **Table 3** shows some of his results.

Table 3

Day	pH
Monday	7.8
Tuesday	7.4
Wednesday	7.0
Thursday	6.9

a On which day is the water in the pool acidic?
(1 mark)

b Give the type of substance that Sam should add to the pool on Monday. Explain your answer.
(2 marks)

c The substance that Sam adds to the pool has the hazard label shown in **Figure 2** on it.

Suggest one safety precaution that Sam should take when using this substance. *(1 mark)*

Figure 2

8 🔬🔬🔬 Many barbecues use charcoal as a fuel. Charcoal is mainly carbon. Carbon burns in air to make carbon dioxide, which is in the gas state at room temperature.

a Define the term 'fuel'. *(1 mark)*

b Suggest whether the burning reaction is exothermic or endothermic, and explain your decision. *(1 mark)*

c Predict whether the mass of solid on the barbecue will increase, decrease, or stay the same. Explain your answer. *(2 marks)*

9 🔬🔬🔬 Describe the differences and similarities between evaporating and boiling. Use the particle model to explain the differences. *(6 marks)*

10 🔺🔺🔺 **Table 4** shows some properties and uses of three elements.

Table 4

Element	Melting point (°C)	Boiling point (°C)	State at 20 °C	Appearance	Other properties	Uses
mercury	−39	357		Shiny and silver-coloured	Does not react with substances in the air	Tilt switches, which set off an alarm if someone shakes a vending machine
platinum	1769	4530		Shiny and silver-coloured	Does not react with substances in the air	Jewellery, catalytic converters in cars, hard disks in computers
silver	961	2210		Shiny and silver-coloured	Reacts with hydrogen sulfide in polluted air to make black silver sulfide	Jewellery and ornaments

a Complete the table by writing down the state of each element at room temperature, 20 °C.

(1 mark)

b Compare the properties of mercury, platinum, and silver. *(3 marks)*

_____

_____

_____

_____

_____

_____

_____

c Using the information given in the table, explain why silver and platinum are used to make jewellery. *(1 mark)*

_____

d Suggest one advantage of using platinum to make jewellery, compared to silver. *(1 mark)*

_____

_____

_____

_____

_____

e A tilt switch sets off an alarm when a vending machine is shaken, or turns off an electric heater if it falls over.

Identify the one property that is different for mercury and platinum that makes mercury suitable for making tilt switches while platinum is unsuitable. *(1 mark)*

_____

_____

f The formula of silver sulfide is Ag_2S. Explain what this formula shows. *(2 marks)*

_____

_____

_____

_____

_____

_____

g At room temperature, sulfur is a yellow solid and silver sulfide is a black solid.
Explain why the properties of silver sulfide are different from the properties of silver and sulfur. *(1 mark)*

_____

_____

h 248 g of silver sulfide contains 216 g of silver. Calculate the percentage by mass of **sulfur** in the compound. Show your working. *(3 marks)*

_____

C1 Checklist

Revision question	Outcome	Topic reference	🙁	😐	🙂
1a	State what a compound is.	C2.3			
1b	Write and interpret chemical formulae.	C2.4			
1c	Write word equations to represent chemical reactions.	C3.2			
2a, b	Write and interpret chemical formulae.	C2.4			
2c	Use the pH scale to measure acidity and alkalinity.	C4.2			
2d	Interpret melting point data to explain the particle movement of different substances at given temperatures.	C1.3			
2e	Discuss the change in particle movement during heating, using particle diagrams to help.	C1.3 C1.4			
3a	State what an element is.	C2.1			
3b	Use the Periodic table to find out chemical symbols.	C2.1			
3c	Use a particle model to explain subliming.	C1.5			
3d	Identify chemical reactions and physical changes.	C3.1			
4a	Identify decomposition reactions from word equations.	C3.4			
4b	Interpret hazard symbols and use them to explain decisions.	WS1.2			
4ci	Use ideas about particles to explain properties of a substance.	C1.2			
4cii	Calculate masses of reactants and products.	C3.5			
4d	Write a balanced formula equation.	C3.2, C3.5			
5a	Name the acid needed to make a given salt.	C4.4			
5b	Identify neutralisation reactions from word equations.	C4.3			
5c	Write word equations to represent chemical reactions.	C3.2			
5d	Convert word equations into formula equations.	C3.2			
5e, f	Use practical techniques to make a salt.	C4.4			
5g	Suggest how to carry out a practical safely.	WS1.2			
6a	State what a base is.	C4.3			
6b	Identify an outlier in a set of data.	C1.3, WS1.4			
6c, d	Calculate a mean from three repeat measurements. Present data appropriately as data and graphs.	WS1.3 🧮			
6e	Interpret data to draw conclusions.	WS1.4			
7a	Use the pH scale to measure acidity and alkalinity.	C4.2			
7b	State how to neutralise a solution of given pH.	C4.3			
7c	Suggest how to carry out a practical safely.	WS1.2			
8a	State what a fuel is.	C3.3			
8b	Classify changes as exothermic or endothermic.	C3.6			
8c	Given information, predict and explain whether the mass within a reaction vessel will stay the same.	C3.5			
9	Explain the differences between evaporation and boiling.	C1.5			
10a	Interpret melting point and boiling point data to decide the state of a substance at a given temperature.	C1.3 C1.4			
10b	Compare the properties and uses of different elements.	C2.1			
10c, d, e	Explain why certain elements are used for given roles, in terms of the properties of the elements.	C2.1			
10f	Write and interpret chemical formulae.	C2.4			
10g	Use the particle model to explain why a compound has different properties to the elements in it.	C2.3			
10h	Calculate the percentage of a given element within a compound.	C2.4 🧮			

P1.1 Introduction to forces

A Fill in the gaps to complete the sentences.

A force can be a _____ or a _____. Forces explain why objects _____

in the way that they do. They can change the _____ that objects are moving in, and change their

_____. They might be a non-contact force, such as _____, or a contact force, such as

_____ or _____. Forces always come in pairs, called _____ pairs. Forces

can be _____ with a newtonmeter. All forces are measured in _____.

B Draw a line to match each sentence's start to a correct middle and ending.

| A force of friction | of the Earth on the water | helps a skydiver land safely. |

| A force of air resistance | of the road on the tyre | makes spilt water spread into a puddle. |

| A force of gravity | of the air on their parachute | makes a bus change speed. |

C Explain the difference between a contact force, such as air resistance, and a non-contact force, such as gravity.

_____

_____

_____

D A fridge magnet is a decorative item that sticks to the side of a fridge, often to hold paper or photographs in place.

a Suggest which forces you think are acting on the magnet. For each of them, draw and label a force arrow on this diagram.

magnet

fridge door

b Choose **one** of the forces on the magnet, and suggest which force completes its interaction pair.

Force: _____

Force that completes the pair: _____

P1.2 Squashing and stretching

A Fill in the gaps to complete the sentences.

Forces can change the shape of objects, or _____ them. Forces can _____ (squash) or stretch objects. When you stand on the floor, your weight compresses the bonds between the particles in the floor. They push back and the floor _____ up on you when you stand on it. This support force from the floor is called the _____ force. Bungee cords, springs, and even lift cables all _____ when you exert a force on them. The amount that they stretch is called the _____. A bungee cord will pull back on the person with a force called _____. Springs are special: if you double the force on a spring, the extension will _____. This relationship is called _____ _____ and it is a _____ relationship. At some point the spring will not go back to its original length when you remove the force. This is the _____ limit.

B A spring is found to obey Hooke's Law. It stretches by 1.2 cm when a force of 50 N is applied. Calculate its extension when a force of 200 N is applied.

_____ cm

C Complete the table for each situation below, describing the effect on the object and giving an explanation for that effect. The first one is completed for you.

Situation	Description of effect on object	Explanation
Cushion supporting a person	Cushion is compressed	Weight of person pushes down, support force from cushion pushes up
Cable supporting a lift		
A bicycle tyre		

D Explain how a solid floor provides a support force to stop you falling towards the Earth. Use scientific terminology and the concept of bonding.

_____

_____

_____

_____

P1.3 Drag forces and friction

A Fill in the gaps to complete the sentences.

_____ grips objects because, although their surfaces might look smooth, they are actually

_____ . One way to reduce friction is to use _____ . Drag forces, such as

_____ resistance or _____ resistance, happen because an object has to push air or

water molecules out of the way. Making an object more _____ is a way to reduce drag. If no other

force is applied, friction and drag forces cause an object to _____ _____ or stop.

B Complete the table to describe the role of friction or drag forces in each situation.

	Situation	Role of friction or drag forces
a	A boat when its engine stops.	
b	A mechanic putting oil on a bicycle chain.	
c	Walking forwards on a pavement.	
d	A skydiver opening her parachute.	

C For each question below, describe the change to each object's motion.

Explain in detail which forces cause each change and why they are acting.

a A boat is crossing a lake. When the engine is cut, the boat's motion changes.

_____

_____

_____

b Someone is pushing a box across a smooth wooden floor. When they stop pushing, the box's motion changes.

_____

_____

_____

D A physicist plans an experiment to investigate the effect of the type of surface on the force required to pull a shoe across it. They will put a 10 kg mass inside the shoe and pull it across a cement paving slab that is horizontal. Then, using the same shoe, they are going to pull it across a sheet of ice that is horizontal.

Identify the following variables:

Independent variable _____

Dependent variable _____

One of the control variables _____

P1.4 Forces at a distance

A Fill in the gaps to complete the sentences.

_____ are regions where an object experiences a _____ force, such as gravitational, magnetic, or electrostatic forces. For instance, around a _____ there is an electrostatic field. If another _____ comes into that field, it experiences a force, and the force gets _____ the closer it comes.

Every object exerts a _____ force on every other object. It increases with mass and _____ with distance. Weight is the force of _____ on an object. You can calculate weight using the equation:

weight (N) = _____ (kg) x gravitational field strength, g (N/kg)

B Circle the correct **bold** phrases in the sentences below.

A field is a region where something experiences **an acceleration / friction / a force**. Around the Earth there is a gravitational field where **magnets / masses / electrical charges** experience a force due to gravity. As an object gets further from the Earth, the field **stays the same / gets stronger / gets weaker**, so that the force on the object becomes smaller.

C The table shows the strength of the gravitational field in different places. A value of 1 N/kg means that a mass of 1 kg experiences a gravitational force (a weight) of 1 N. An astronaut and her equipment have a mass of 160 kg. Complete the table by calculating the weight of the astronaut in each place.

Place	Gravitational field strength (N/kg)	Weight of astronaut and her equipment (N)
the Earth's surface	9.8	
in orbit around the Earth	8.7	
the Moon's surface	1.6	
far from any star or planet	0.0	

D Lightning is caused by charges in a thundercloud creating an electrostatic field.

Suggest why it is more dangerous to stand on a high building than on the ground during a thunderstorm.

_____

_____

E The Voyager 1 space probe was launched in 1977. It has been travelling away from the Earth and Sun ever since, and is now the most distant man-made object.

Describe and explain any changes to the gravitational force on the probe due to the Earth.

_____

_____

_____

P1.5 Balanced and unbalanced

A Fill in the gaps to complete the sentences.

Sometimes the forces on an object are _____, so that it is in _____. The object's motion will not change – if it was already moving, it will continue in the same _____ at the same _____. If it was not moving, it will stay still. If the forces are _____ then the object's motion will change its _____ and/or _____.

B Describe two situations that are in equilibrium, identifying the forces involved and what condition is true about them.

1 _____

_____

2 _____

_____

C **a** Add force arrows to this diagram to show balanced forces.

b Add force arrows to this diagram to show unbalanced forces.

c Explain the difference between balanced and unbalanced forces using your examples.

_____

_____

_____

D **a** Draw and label one or more force arrows on this diagram.

b Explain why the Moon orbits the Earth in circles.

_____

_____

_____

_____

_____

orbit

Moon

Earth

P1 Chapter 1 Pinchpoint

Pinchpoint question

Answer the question below, then do the follow-up activity **with the same letter** as the answer you picked.

A bicycle is turning a corner to the left. It is changing direction but not speed.

Circle which diagram and statement best describes the situation.

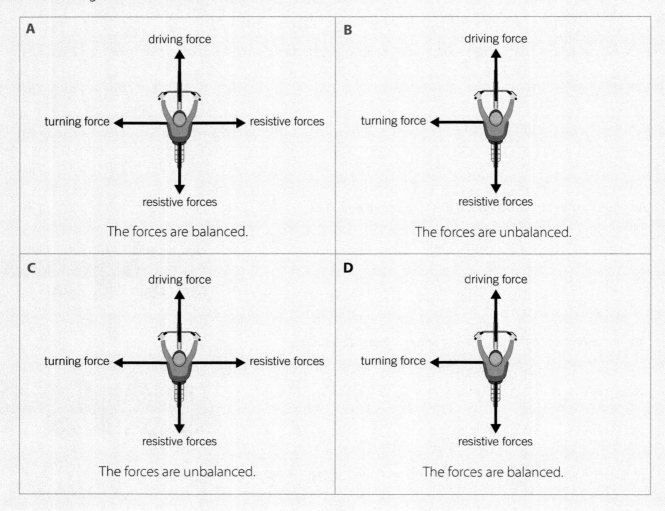

A
driving force
turning force ← → resistive forces
resistive forces
The forces are balanced.

B
driving force
turning force ←
resistive forces
The forces are unbalanced.

C
driving force
turning force ← → resistive forces
resistive forces
The forces are unbalanced.

D
driving force
turning force ←
resistive forces
The forces are balanced.

Follow-up activities

A Forces must be unbalanced to change an object's motion.

   a Marianne holds a ball in her hand. There are two forces acting on the ball.

     i Draw and label their force arrows on this diagram.

     ii Are the forces balanced? _____

     iii Is the motion of the ball changing? _____

b She now takes her hand away, dropping the ball. Think about which forces – if any – are now acting on the ball.

    i Draw and label force arrows – if any – on this diagram.

    ii Are the forces balanced? _____

    iii Is the motion of the ball changing? _____

Hint: Can balanced forces change motion? For help see P1 1.5 Balanced and unbalanced.

B To move in a circle, an object must have an unbalanced force acting on it, pointing in a particular direction.

    a A cyclist rides around a roundabout. Draw on the diagram the direction of the turning force.

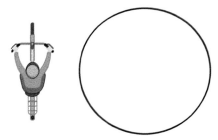

    b The cyclist continues around the roundabout. Draw on the diagram the direction of the turning force.

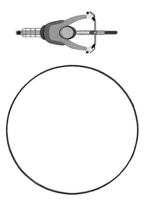

Hint: Is turning a corner a change in motion? For help see P1 1.5 Balanced and unbalanced.

C Every force has an interaction pair, but for unbalanced forces, the paired force is on a **different** object.

In the example of the turning cyclist in the Pinchpoint question, the turning force is the road pushing the cyclist to the left.

a Give the other force in that interaction pair. _____

b The diagram below shows someone pushing a box, showing the arrow for that force.

Draw a force arrow to show the interaction pair for the person pushing a box.

c Which object is your force arrow acting on? _____

Hint: What is the definition of balanced forces? For help see P1 1.5 Balanced and unbalanced.

D Motion cannot change for an object with balanced forces on it. Forces must be unbalanced to change motion.

For each diagram below:

- write whether the forces are **balanced** or **unbalanced**,
- write whether motion will **change** or **not** change
- if motion will change, write whether the object will turn **left** or **right**, **speed up**, or **slow down**.

Force arrows diagram	Balanced or unbalanced?	Motion will change or not change?	If motion will change, turn left, turn right, speed up, or slow down?
a			
b			
c			
d			

Hint: What is the definition of balanced forces? For help see P1 1.5 Balanced and unbalanced.

⊗ Pinchpoint review

Now look back at the question – do you think you chose the right letter?
Turn to the Answers page to find out.

A Fill in the gaps to complete the sentences.

In science, a _____ is an oscillation or vibration that transfers _____ or information. _____ is the distance from the middle to the top of a wave. _____ is the number of waves that go past a particular point per second. _____ is the distance from one point on a wave to the same point on the next wave. The top of a wave is called a _____ or crest, and the bottom of a wave is called a _____. In a _____ wave, the oscillation is at 90° to the direction of the wave. In a _____ wave, the oscillation is parallel to the direction of the wave. When considering a slinky spring, in a compression the coils of the spring are _____ _____. In a rarefaction the coils are _____ _____. Waves bounce off surfaces and barriers. This is called _____. The wave coming into the barrier is called the _____ wave and the wave bouncing off the barrier is called the _____ wave.

B a Label the diagram of the wave.

b Identify the type of wave shown. _____

C Give **one** similarity and **one** difference between transverse and longitudinal waves.

Similarity: _____

Difference: _____

D a Explain what happens when a water wave or a sound wave hits a hard surface.

_____

_____

b Two water waves from different directions reach a point at the same time.
Describe and explain **one** possible effect due to superposition.

_____

_____

P2.2 Sound and energy transfer

A Fill in the gaps to complete the sentences.

An object must _____ to cause a sound wave. As it moves backwards and forwards, it causes

_____ in the medium to do the same. Sound needs a medium, whether solid, liquid, or gas, to travel

through. It cannot travel through a _____. Sound travels fastest in a _____ – this is

because the particles in a solid are closer together than in a liquid or a gas, so the vibration is passed along more

_____. _____ travels almost a million times faster than sound and does not need a

_____ to travel through.

B Explain why the speed of sound in solids is different from the speed of sound in gases, using each of the following keywords at least once.

vibration	medium	solid	gas	sound wave	faster	particles

_____

_____

_____

_____

C Concorde was a **supersonic** passenger plane that operated until 2003. Several aeroplane manufacturers are currently trying to develop a new one. Explain what supersonic travel means.

_____

D Some fireworks use an explosion to produce a bright flash and a loud bang.

Compare and explain the time taken for an observer to hear and see the explosion of a firework.

_____

_____

E We can see the Sun (on a cloudless day). Explain why we will never hear the Sun on Earth.

_____

_____

_____

P2.3 Loudness and pitch

A Fill in the gaps to complete the sentences.

A loud sound has a bigger _____ than a quieter sound. A sound with high pitch has a higher

_____, which is measured in _____ (Hz). Humans cannot hear sound waves with a

frequency below _____ Hz; these are called _____. Humans cannot hear sound waves

with a frequency above 20 000 Hz; these are called _____. The range of frequencies that a human

or an animal can hear is called the _____ range. Many animals can hear frequencies that are much

_____ than the frequencies we can hear.

B Describe how the range of hearing in humans differs from that in other animals.

_____

_____

C a On the grid below, sketch a louder wave than the one shown.

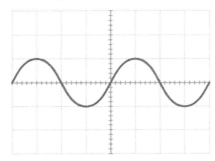

b On the grid below, sketch a lower-pitched wave than the one shown.

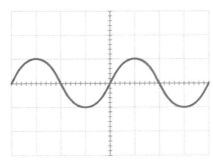

D The table shows the hearing range for several species, including humans.

Explain what each species would hear if there was a sound wave of 1000 Hz.

Species	Hearing range (Hz)	What will they hear for 1000 Hz sound wave?	Reason
Human	20–20 000		
Bat	2000–110 000		
Dog	67–45 000		

P2.4 Detecting sound

A Fill in the gaps to complete the sentences.

Your _____ detects sound waves by the outer ear or _____ collecting the waves and directing them along the _____ canal to the middle ear where the _____ vibrates. These vibrations pass to the _____, tiny bones that _____ the sound and pass the vibration through the oval window to the inner ear or _____. Here the liquid and _____ cells vibrate. Electrical signals are transmitted from here via the auditory _____ to the _____ and you hear the sound. Sound intensity is measured in _____ (dB). Exposure to very loud sounds can permanently _____ the hair cells in the cochlea so that you can become deaf.

A microphone has a flexible plate called a _____ that vibrates, producing an _____ signal. Loudspeakers vibrate, converting the electrical signal back to sound via an _____ to make the sound louder.

B Describe how each of the following parts of the ear helps you to hear.

a Ossicles _____

b Auditory nerve _____

C Sound is a wave. Explain how the following parts of the ear transfer vibrations to help you hear.

a Pinna _____

b Eardrum _____

c Cochlea _____

D Imagine you work for a construction company that uses noisy equipment.

Write a short note for the employees explaining how their hearing can be damaged. Explain two factors that affect their risk, with at least one action they can take for each.

_____

_____

_____

_____

_____

E Give and explain one similarity and one difference between the ear and the microphone.

Similarity _____

_____

Difference _____

_____

A Fill in the gaps to complete the sentences.

_____ is sound waves with a frequency too high for humans to hear, above _____ Hz. It can be used for things like _____, where a beam of ultrasound is sent out by a _____ under a ship. It travels through the water and _____ off the seabed. A _____ detects the reflection and measures the _____ it took to transmit and receive the reflection from the seabed. That allows us to work out how deep the sea must be. The reflection of a sound is called an _____. If lots of _____ join together to produce a longer sound, this is called a _____.

B **a** Describe what ultrasound is.

_____

_____

   b Explain how ultrasound can be analysed so that a doctor can make images of an unborn baby.

_____

_____

_____

_____

   c Name and explain one use of ultrasound, other than medical imaging.

_____

_____

C Name one way that an animal uses echolocation. Explain why they use it, and how it works.

_____

_____

_____

Pinchpoint question

Answer the question below, then do the follow-up activity **with the same letter** as the answer you picked.

Here is a sound wave shown on the screen of an oscilloscope.

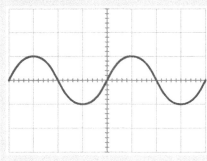

Which of the three sound waves, **X**, **Y**, and **Z** below, have a **higher pitch** than the sound wave above?

X

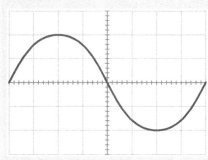

Y

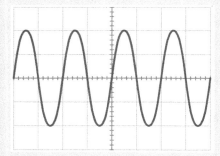

Z

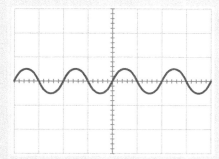

A   **X** and **Y**

B   **X** only

C   **Y** and **Z**

D   **Z** only

A The **loudness** of a sound relates to its amplitude: a **louder** sound has a wave that has a **larger** distance vertically from centre to peak and centre to trough.

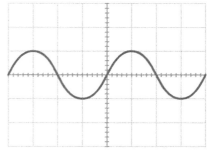

The **pitch** of a sound relates to its frequency: a **higher**-pitched sound has a wave that has a **higher** frequency so there are more waves (shown by more peaks) in the same time interval.

Here is a sound wave shown on the screen of an oscilloscope:

a Compared to the sound wave on the right, which of the sound waves below, **Q** or **R**, is louder?

_____

Q

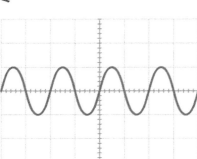

R

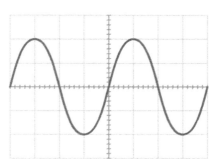

b Which of the sound waves, **Q** or **R**, has a higher pitch? _____

Hint: Does pitch relate to amplitude or frequency? For help see P1 2.3 Loudness and pitch.

B The pitch of a sound relates to its frequency: a **higher** pitched sound has a wave that has a **higher** frequency.

In the two sound waves below, wave **S** has a higher frequency and therefore a higher pitch than wave **T**.

S

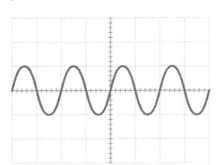

T

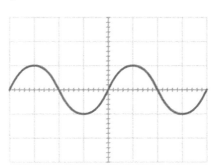

Describe **one** difference you can see in the waves **S** and **T** that shows you that sound wave **S** has a higher pitch than sound wave **T**.

Hint: Are the waves in a higher-pitched sound closer together or further apart? For help see P1 2.3 Loudness and pitch.

_____

_____

C Light has some similar properties to sound. The frequency of light relates to its colour, for example, violet light has a higher frequency than red light. The brightness of light relates to its amplitude, for example, bright violet light has a higher amplitude than dim violet light.

Wave **U** below represents a bright, red light. On the blank oscilloscope screen below, sketch a wave to represent a dim, violet light.

U

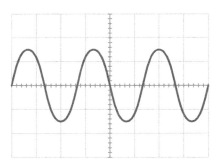 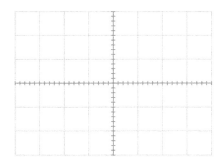

Hint: To which properties of a wave do brightness and colour relate? For help with this follow-up activity, see P1 3.5 Colour.

D a On the waves **V** and **W** below, label the amplitude and wavelength for each one.

V   **W**

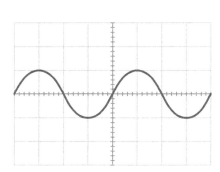 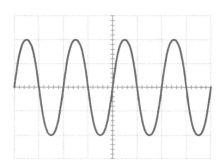

b Wave **W** has a higher frequency than wave **V**. How big is wave **W**'s wavelength compared to wave **V**?

_____

Hint: Does higher pitch mean higher or lower frequency? For help see P1 2.3 Loudness and pitch.

Pinchpoint review

Now look back at the question – do you think you chose the right letter?
Turn to the Answers page to find out.

P3.1 Light

A Fill in the gaps to complete the sentences.

_____ objects emit light: they are a _____ of light. Most objects are _____ -

_____ – they do not emit light. You can see objects when light is _____ off them and

absorbed by your _____. Transparent substances _____ light. _____

substances do not. _____ substances transmit light, but it is _____. Light travels as a

_____ through gases, some liquids like water, and some solids like glass. It can even travel through

empty space, called a _____. The speed of light is about _____ m/s. Astronomers

use '_____-_____' to measure distances in space.

B The statements below can be reordered to describe the process of seeing the Moon.
Read the statements and write down the order of statements that you think will give the best description.

Correct order: ☐ ☐ ☐ ☐ ☐

1 The Moon is a non-luminous object.

2 Some of the reflected light is absorbed in your eye.

3 It does not emit light itself, it just reflects light from the Sun.

4 The Sun is a luminous object.

5 It is a source of light – it emits light waves through space.

C There is a cat playing outside a window. You are looking at the cat in daylight.
Suggest how light interacts with each of the following.

a Cat _____

b Glass in window _____

c Back of your eye _____

D a Light has a speed of 300 000 km/s. Calculate the distance, in km, that it would travel in one year.

Distance = _____ km

Hint: Speed is the distance travelled in one second. How many seconds are there in one minute? Minutes in an hour? Hours in a day? Days in a year?

b The nearest star to Earth, other than the Sun, is Proxima Centauri. It is 4.2 light-years from Earth.
Calculate that distance in km.

Distance = _____ km

P3.2 Reflection

A Fill in the gaps to complete the sentences.

Light _____ off a mirror in the same way that a wave _____ off a barrier. The light

that hits the mirror is called the _____ ray. The reflected light is called the _____

ray. An imaginary line at 90° to the mirror is called the _____. You measure angles from the normal

to the rays of light. Rays reflect from surfaces with an angle of reflection _____ to the angle of

_____. This is called the law of _____. With a flat or _____ mirror, the

surface is smooth, causing _____ reflection; the reflected rays give a _____ image,

as if there is someone the same shape and size as you the other side of the mirror. With a rough surface, there is

_____ scattering, where no image is visible.

B **a** Write down how the angle of reflection relates to the angle of incidence.

_____

b The diagram on the right shows one form of reflection.
Does it show specular reflection or diffuse scattering? _____

c Explain how the law of reflection causes this form of reflection.

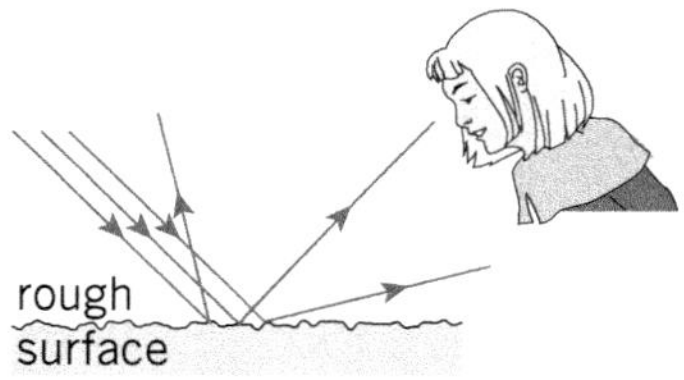

_____

_____

_____

rough
surface

C Someone looks at the reflection of a candle in a plane mirror. Draw a ray diagram showing how an image is formed.

D Use the concepts of specular reflection and diffuse scattering to explain the following.

a On a sunny day, a room with windows appears bright inside even if you are not sitting in direct sunlight.

_____

_____

_____

b Sometimes outside on a sunny day you will see very bright bits of light when passing cars and the windows of buildings.

_____

_____

_____

P3.3 Refraction

A Fill in the gaps to complete the sentences.

When light passes from one _____ into another it changes _____. This causes

it to change _____; a process called _____. If light goes from air into glass it

_____ _____ and bends _____ the normal. This effect makes swimming

pools appear _____ than they are. The effect can be used to produce _____ or convex

lenses which bring light to a _____ or focal point.

B **a** If you are above a pond looking down at a stone, the stone appears to be nearer the surface than it really is. Explain why this happens.

_____

_____

_____

b Complete this ray diagram that illustrates the scenario described in part **a**, showing how the two rays refract to form an image.

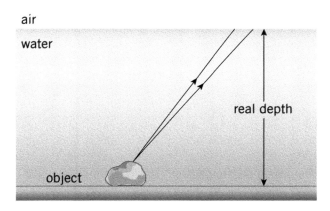

C **a** Draw a ray diagram to show how a converging lens forms an image.

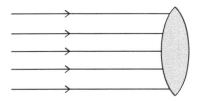

b Explain what happens when light travels through a converging lens so that an image is formed.

_____

_____

_____

P3.4 The eye and the camera

A Fill in the gaps to complete the sentences.

Your eye works by _____ light reflected from an _____ you are looking at. Your cornea

and _____ focus the light. Your _____ controls the size of your _____,

letting through more or less light. A real (not virtual) inverted image is formed on your _____ where

_____ absorb the light, causing _____ reactions which send electrical signals along

the _____ nerve to your brain. Digital and pinhole cameras produce real images in a similar way. In a

digital camera, there is a grid of photosensitive _____ called a charge-coupled device (CCD). When

light hits each _____ they free _____ charges.

B Draw a line to match each part in the left-hand column with its function.

object	A hole that allows light to enter the lens.
cornea and lens	Controls the size of the pupil, allowing in more or less light.
iris	Real (you could put a screen here and you would see an image), inverted, smaller than the object.
pupil	Where the image forms – contains photoreceptors.
retina	Reflected light from this enters the eye.
photoreceptors	Rods and cones – absorb light causing a chemical reaction which produces an electrical signal.
image	Sends electrical signal to the brain.
optic nerve	Focus the light.

C Explain how the eye forms an image. In your explanation, include whether the image is real or virtual, inverted or not, and larger or smaller than the object being viewed.

_____

_____

_____

D Compare a simple camera with the eye.

_____

_____

_____

_____

A Fill in the gaps to complete the sentences.

Our eyes detect three _____ colours of light: red, green, and blue. Two of these colours of light

added together make _____ colours of light, for instance blue and green light added together

make _____ light. All three _____ colours of light added together make

_____ light. Filters _____ light; for instance, a blue filter _____ all

colours except _____ from white light.

Coloured objects subtract light by _____ only their own colour. For example, a blue object appears

blue because when white light falls on it, all colours are absorbed except _____, which reflects.

A _____ can be used to split up light into a _____ of different colours. It does this

because of _____: light with the highest _____ (violet) refracts more than light with

the _____ frequency (red). The spectrum from the Sun's light is _____ – it has no gaps.

B Explain why a prism forms a spectrum.

_____

_____

_____

C Explain how primary colours are combined to form the secondary colour yellow.

_____

_____

_____

D a A white object is illuminated by red light and viewed through a green filter.

Suggest and explain how it will appear.

_____

_____

_____

b A green object is illuminated by white light and viewed through a green filter.

Suggest and explain how it will appear.

_____

_____

_____

E A red ball is illuminated using yellow light. Suggest and explain how it will appear.

_____

_____

_____

Pinchpoint question

Answer the question below, then do the follow-up activity **with the same letter** as the answer you picked.

A ray of light is travelling in glass.
Choose the ray diagram below that correctly shows what happens when the ray hits the edge of the glass.

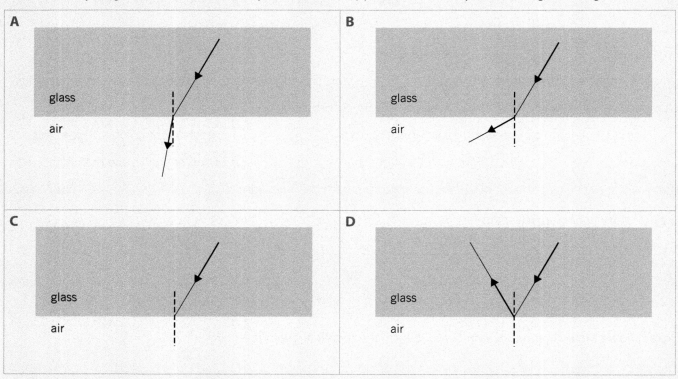

Follow-up activities

A **a** Does light travel faster or slower in glass compared to air? _____

b In your own words, write down the rules that light rays obey during refraction. Use each of the following keywords at least once.

medium	towards	away	normal	faster	slower	refracts

_____

_____

_____

Hint: Which way does light refract when moving from one transparent medium to another? For help see P1 3.3 Refraction.

B Use the concept of refraction to explain the appearance of this spoon through the water.

_____

_____

_____

_____

_____

_____

Hint: When will a light ray refract? For help see P1 3.3 Refraction.

C Complete the sentences using these keywords.

slower	absorbed	faster	slower	refract
normal	transmitted	faster	scattered	

Light can interact with matter in different ways. It will be _____ in an opaque material. It will be

_____ in a translucent material. It will be _____ through a transparent material.

When passing from one transparent medium into another, the behaviour depends on the speed of light in those

materials. It will _____ towards the _____ going from a medium in which it is

_____ (such as air) into one where it is _____ (such as glass). It will refract away from

the normal going from a medium in which it is _____ into one where it is _____.

Hint: When will a light ray refract? For help see P1 3.3 Refraction.

D Complete the following sentences using these keywords.

transmitted	speeds up	mirror	reflected
away from	refracts	towards	slows down

A _____ is a smooth sheet of metallic, opaque material (often behind a sheet of glass to protect it).

Light is _____ from mirrors; it is not _____. It _____ when it passes from

one transparent medium into another. When a light ray passes from air into glass, it will bend _____

the normal as it _____. It will bend _____ the normal when passing from water into

air as it _____.

Hint: When will a light ray refract? For help see P1 3.3 Refraction.

 Pinchpoint review

Now look back at the question – do you think you chose the right letter?
Turn to the Answers page to find out.

P4.1 The night sky

A Fill in the gaps to complete the sentences.

We can see many different objects in the night sky without a telescope. The nearest are artificial

_____ that _____ the Earth. The _____ is the Earth's only

_____ satellite. We can also see five _____: Mercury, Venus, _____,

Jupiter, and Saturn. Like Earth, they orbit the _____ and make up part of the _____

_____. We may also be lucky enough to see meteors or _____ in the night sky. The dots

of light we see are _____ in our own _____, which is called the _____

_____. It is just one of billions of galaxies that make up the _____.

B Describe and define each of the following.

a Meteor _____

b Solar system _____

c Galaxy _____

d Star _____

C Match each object with its distance from Earth.

Proxima Centauri – nearest star (other than the Sun)	2 million light-years
Moon	8 light-minutes
Andromeda – nearest large galaxy (other than the Milky Way)	4 light-years
Sun	1 light-second

D Describe the structure of the Universe in detail, in order of size starting with the smallest objects.
Include the following keywords:

asteroids	Milky Way	Universe	moons	Sun	planets	Solar System

_____

_____

_____

_____

_____

P4.2 The Solar System

A Fill in the gaps to complete the sentences.

At the centre of the _____ System is the _____. It is orbited by four inner

_____ and four outer _____. Each orbit is a squashed circle shape called an

_____. The inner planets are Mercury, _____, Earth, and _____. They

are all terrestrial planets; they are made of _____. The outer planets are Jupiter, Saturn, Uranus, and

Neptune. They are called _____ giants; they are made mainly of _____ and are very

cold and much bigger than the inner planets. Many planets have _____ that orbit them. Between

the inner and outer planets there is an _____ belt made up of thousands of pieces of rock. Pluto

used to be called a planet but is now called a _____ planet.

B Draw a line to match each object with its description.

asteroid belt	made up of ice and dust; sometimes orbits close to the Sun, sometimes far
Sun	orbits Sun, may be rocky or gas giant
a planet	orbits a planet
a moon	made up of small rocky bodies, between Mars and Jupiter
a comet	in the centre of the Solar System

C Look at the data in the table for the first seven planets in the Solar System.

Planet	Diameter (km)	Distance from Sun (millions of km)	Temperature (°C)	Composition	Number of moons	Has rings
Mercury	4800	58	−180 to 430	Rocky	0	No
Venus	12 000	110	470	Rocky	0	No
Earth	13 000	150	−89 to 58	Rocky	1	No
Mars	6800	230	−82 to 0	Rocky	2	No
Jupiter	140 000	780	−150	Gas giant	67	Yes
Saturn	120 000	1400	−170	Gas giant	62	Yes
Uranus	51 000	2900	−200	Gas giant	27	Yes

a Explain how the properties and features of planets are linked to their place in the Solar System.

_____

_____

_____

_____

b An eighth planet, Neptune, was discovered beyond Uranus, orbiting at 4500 million km from the Sun.
Use the data in the table to predict the features and properties of Neptune.

_____

_____

D Give two similarities and two differences in the orbit and composition between an asteroid and a planet.

Similarity 1 _____

Similarity 2 _____

Difference 1 _____

Difference 2 _____

P4.3 The Earth

A Fill in the gaps to complete the sentences.

Once each _____, the Earth _____ on its axis, causing the Sun's apparent motion

through the sky and giving us day and _____. Once each _____, the Earth

_____ around the Sun. The differences between summer and winter in the UK are mainly caused

by the _____ of the Earth's axis. In summer, the Northern Hemisphere tilts _____

the Sun, which means that each bit of the ground receives _____ of the Sun's rays; days are

_____, and the Sun appears to rise _____ into the sky at noon.

B Draw a line to match the object with the description and explanation of the apparent movement of the object in the sky.

| the Moon | | the Earth orbits the Sun once a year and the night-side of the Earth faces different constellations of stars during the year |

| the Sun | | the Earth spins on its axis once every 24 hours and so different regions of the Earth face the Sun at different times of day |

| stars | | orbits the Earth once a month |

C Consider the data in the table below.

City, country	Latitude (degrees north of equator)	Daylight hours on 'longest' day (hours)
Accra, Ghana	5	
Rabat, Morocco	34	14.4
Plymouth, UK	50	16.4
Aberdeen, UK	57	17.9
Iqaluit, Canada	63	

a Predict how the average temperatures in these cities compare during summer in the northern hemisphere. Give a reason for your answer.

_____

_____

_____

_____

b Use the data above to predict the number of daylight hours in Accra and Iqaluit on the longest day.

Accra: _____ hours

Iqaluit: _____ hours

D Suggest how seasons in a temperate country, such as the UK, would be different if the Earth's axis of rotation was not tilted.

_____

_____

_____

P4.4 The Moon

A Fill in the gaps to complete the sentences.

_____ of the Moon is lit by the _____ at all times. As it orbits the _____

we see different amounts of it illuminated by the Sun, causing the _____ of the Moon. When the side

facing the Earth is in shadow, we call it a _____ moon. Later, when we see the whole of the side lit by

the Sun, we call it a _____ moon. This cycle occurs once each lunar _____.

If the Moon is between the _____ and the _____, a shadow called the

_____ occurs on Earth, where the light from the Sun is totally blocked and there will be a total

_____ eclipse. The _____ occurs where only part of the Sun's light is blocked and a

partial _____ eclipse occurs. If the Earth comes between the Sun and the _____ and

blocks the Sun's light from reaching the Moon, a _____ eclipse can occur.

B Look at the diagram of the Moon orbiting the Earth.

For each position 1–8 on the diagram, write down a letter A–H in the table below, to show which phase of the Moon is seen by someone on Earth.

Position				1	2	3	4	5	6	7	8
Phase of the Moon (A–H)											

C Imagine that a particular lunar month has 28 days, so that on day 1 there is a new moon.
Predict which phase occurs for each of the days listed in the table.

Day of lunar month	Phase of the moon
8	
15	
22	
26	
29	

D a Explain how total solar eclipses and total lunar eclipses happen.

   i Total solar eclipse: _____

   ii Total lunar eclipse: _____

 b Explain which phase the Moon is in when each type of eclipse occurs.

   i Total solar eclipse: _____

   ii Total lunar eclipse: _____

E Explain why it is possible to see an eclipse on some of the planets in the Solar System but not on others.

_____

_____

_____

Hint: What is required for an eclipse to occur?

P1 Chapter 4 Pinchpoint

Pinchpoint question

Answer the question below, then do the follow-up activity **with the same letter** as the answer you picked.

Astronomers have been able to work out where objects are in the Universe.

Which of these statements is true?

A The Sun orbits the Earth in our Solar System.

B Our Solar System is made up of a star with planets that orbit it.

C The order of scale (smallest to largest) is Earth, Sun, Milky Way, Solar System, Universe.

D The Milky Way is a galaxy in our Solar System.

Follow-up activities

A The Earth orbits the Sun.

Name three different types of object which orbit our Sun.

_____

_____

Hint: Which objects are in our Solar System? For help see P1 4.1 The night sky.

B Choose which option correctly indicates the distances from the Earth of: the Moon, the Sun, Proxima Centauri (nearest star beyond the Sun), and Andromeda (nearest galaxy beyond the Milky Way).

Distance from ...	Option 1	Option 2	Option 3
... **Moon to Earth**	500 000× Earth diameter	4× Earth diameter	30× Earth diameter
... **Sun to Earth**	300 000× further away than the Moon	20× further away than the Moon	400× further away than Moon
... **Proxima Centauri to Earth**	400× further away than the Sun	5000× further away than the Sun	300 000× further away than Sun
... **Andromeda to Earth**	30× further away than Proxima Centauri	200× further away than Proxima Centauri	500 000× further away than Proxima Centauri

Hint: What are the light-distances to other objects? For help see P1 4.1 The night sky.

C The Milky Way is our galaxy and consists of billions of stars. Our Solar System consists of the planets orbiting one of those stars – the Sun.

Draw a diagram to show the structure of our Solar System, and which objects orbit which others. Include the following: the Moon, the Earth, Jupiter, and the Sun.

Hint: What do planets orbit? For help see P1 4.1 The night sky.

D The Milky Way is our galaxy and consists of billions of stars. Our Solar System consists of the planets orbiting one of those stars – the Sun.

a Write the order for the objects in the table below, with '1' being the nearest to the Earth.

b Tick each object that is within the Milky Way.

Object	Order (1 is nearest Earth)	✓ if within Milky Way
Proxima Centauri (next nearest star beyond Sun)		
Sun		
Jupiter		
Moon		
Andromeda galaxy		

Hint: Where are the nearest stars? For help see P1 4.1 The night sky.

Pinchpoint review

Now look back at the question – do you think you chose the right letter?
Turn to the Answers page to find out.

P1 Revision questions

1 🧪🧪 A skydiver is falling to Earth with her parachute open.

   a Name a force acting on her which changes with distance. *(1 mark)*

   _____

   _____

   b Identify both forces for one interaction pair involving the skydiver and describe why they are an interaction pair. *(4 marks)*

   _____

   _____

   _____

   _____

   _____

   _____

2 🧪🧪 Give **two** things that forces can change about objects. *(2 marks)*

   1 _____

   2 _____

3 🧪🧪 The speed of sound in air is 340 m/s and in water it is 1500 m/s.
Explain why these are different. *(2 marks)*

   _____

   _____

   _____

   _____

4 🧪🧪 Describe **two** ways that your hearing can be impaired. *(2 marks)*

   _____

   _____

   _____

   _____

5 🧪🧪 Describe **two** similarities and **two** differences between the planets Venus and Jupiter. *(4 marks)*

   Similarities: _____

   _____

   Differences: _____

   _____

6 🧪🧪 **Figure 1** shows the positions of the Moon and some of the stars in the constellations Capricorn and Sagittarius in the night sky.

Figure 1 Day 1, 00:00

Figure 2 shows the same view of the night sky, one hour later.

Figure 2 Day 1, 01:00

Figure 3 shows the same view of the night sky the next night at the same time as **Figure 1**.

Figure 3 Day 2, 00:00

Explain why the positions of the Moon and stars are different in **Figures 2** and **3** compared to **Figure 1**. *(4 marks)*

_____

_____

_____

_____

_____

_____

7 🧪🧪 Waves can be either transverse or longitudinal. Describe the difference between transverse and longitudinal waves. *(2 marks)*

_____

_____

_____

_____

8 🧪🧪 The lighting technician on a film set wants to produce different colours. He requires cyan but only has red, green, and blue lamps available.

  a Describe how he can produce the secondary colour cyan from the primary colours. *(2 marks)*

_____

  b The film set has some coloured glass that acts as a green filter. The technician tests the coloured glass to see whether light will emerge from it for each primary lamp, and if so, what colour light it is. Complete **Table 1** to show his findings. *(3 marks)*

Table 1

Colour of lamp	Does light emerge from glass?	If yes, which colour?
red		
green		
blue		

9 a 🧪🧪 Describe an example of light being refracted, including what happens to the ray of light. *(2 marks)*

_____

_____

  b 🧪🧪 Explain why light is refracted in the example you gave in part **a**. *(1 mark)*

_____

_____

  c 🧪🧪 Complete the ray diagram in **Figure 4** to show what happens when light travels through a converging lens. *(2 marks)*

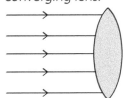

Figure 4

  d 🧪🧪🧪 A physicist learnt about a property of lenses called 'power'. You need a more 'powerful' or stronger spectacle lens if your eyesight is poor. She measured the focal length of lenses of different powers and drew this graph.

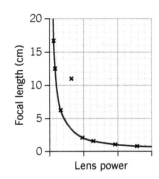

Describe any pattern and any anomalies in this graph. *(3 marks)*

_____

_____

_____

10 🧪🧪🧪 Voyager 1 is the space probe that has travelled furthest from Earth; it is currently leaving the Solar System. Explain how the effect of gravity on its mass and weight changed as it moved away from Earth. *(3 marks)*

_____

_____

_____

11 🧪🧪🧪 A car is parked on a bridge. Describe the interaction pairs acting on the car and on the bridge. *(4 marks)*

_____

_____

_____

_____

12 🧪🧪🧪 A scientist investigates a new material and finds that it obeys Hooke's Law.

  a When she applies a force of 1500 N, she observes that it stretches by 1.2 mm. Predict the extension for a force of 1 N (called the spring constant). *(2 marks)*

_____

  b **Table 2** shows readings that the scientist measured for a similar material. On the axes overleaf, plot the data and draw a line of best fit. *(3 marks)*

Table 2

Force (N)	Extension (mm)
0	0.0
200	0.9
400	1.7
600	2.6
800	3.3
1000	4.0
1200	4.8
1400	5.6
1600	6.6

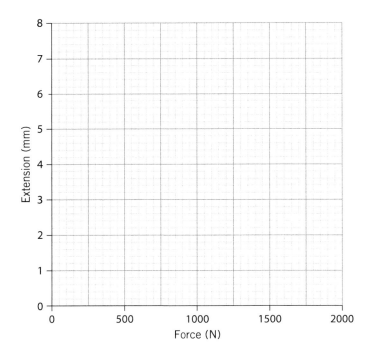

c Describe the relationship between the variables shown in your graph for part **b**. (*1 mark*)

_____

_____

13 🧪🧪🧪 If you bring a magnet close to a piece of iron and let go, the iron and magnet will 'jump' together. When a bird flies, its weight is pulling it down. Compare magnetic and gravitational fields using these examples. (*4 marks*)

_____

_____

_____

_____

14 🧪🧪🧪 Explain how ultrasound can be used in modern life. Include at least one medical and one non-medical use. (*6 marks*)

_____

_____

_____

_____

_____

_____

_____

15 🧪🧪🧪 On the axes below, sketch two waves of different loudness but the same pitch. Label them to indicate which is louder. (*3 marks*)

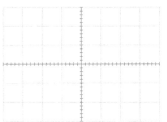

16 🧪🧪🧪 Calculate the distance travelled by light in a light-year. Give your answer in metres. The speed of light is 300 000 000 m/s. A year has 365 days. (*2 marks*)

_____

17 🧪🧪🧪 Some sunlight falls at an angle on two different objects: a transparent window made of glass, and an opaque blue ball. Predict how light will interact with these two objects. (*4 marks*)

_____

_____

_____

_____

18 🧪🧪🧪 In a lunar month of 29 days, the new moon always occurs on day 1. Predict on which day

a the first quarter moon will occur (*1 mark*)

_____

b the first full moon will occur. (*1 mark*)

_____

19 🧪🧪🧪 **Table 3** shows data for two exoplanets, with two planets for comparison. These exoplanets both orbit stars that have similar masses to the Sun. Suggest values for the missing properties for each of the exoplanets and complete the table. (*4 marks*)

Table 3

Planet	Average distance from star it orbits (Earth = 1)	Mass (Earth = 1)	Type of planet
Earth	1.0	1	Rocky
Jupiter	5.2	318	Gas giant
Exoplanet A	0.04		
Exoplanet B	3.6		

P1 Checklist

Revision question	Outcome	Topic reference	😞	😐	😊
1a	State that gravity changes with distance.	P1 1.4			
1b	Describe what is meant by an interaction pair.	P1 1.1			
2	Define equilibrium.	P1 1.5			
3	Explain why the speed of sound is different in different media.	P1 2.2			
4	Describe how your hearing can be damaged.	P1 2.4			
5	Explain the motion of the stars and Moon across the sky.	P1 4.3			
6	Describe some similarities and differences between the planets of the Solar System.	P1 4.2			
7	Describe the different types of wave and their features.	P1 2.1			
8a	Describe how primary colours add to make secondary colours.	P1 3.5			
8b	Predict the colour of objects in red light and the colour of light through different filters.	P1 3.5			
9a, b	Describe and explain what happens when light is refracted.	P1 3.3			
9c	Describe what happens when light travels through a lens.	P1 3.3			
9d	Present data in a graph and recognise quantitative patterns and errors.	P1 1.2			
10	Explain how the effect of gravity changes moving away from the Earth.	P1 1.4			
11	Explain how solid surfaces provide a support force, using scientific terminology and bonding.	P1 1.2			
12a	Apply Hooke's Law to make quantitative predictions with unfamiliar materials.	P1 1.2			
12b, c	Present data in a graph and recognise quantitative patterns and errors.	P1 1.2			
13	Apply the effects of forces at a distance to different fields.	P1 1.4			
14	Explain some uses of ultrasound.	P1 2.5			
15	Compare and contrast waves of different loudness using a diagram.	P1 2.3			
16	Calculate the distance travelled by light in a light-year.	P1 3.1			
17	Predict how light will interact with different materials.	P1 3.1			
18	Predict phases of the Moon at a given time.	P1 4.4			
19	Use data to make predictions about features of planets.	P1 4.2			

Answers

WS1.1 and WS1.2

A question, prediction, knowledge, independent, dependent, control, equipment, risk assessment, data, precise, reproducible

B
  a the variable you change
  b the variable that changes because of the variable you change
  c a variable that must be kept the same during an investigation

C
  a e.g. hair length / height / mass (data that can have any value within a range)
  b e.g. number of insects / number of paperclips picked up by an electromagnet (data that can only have specific numeric values)
  c e.g. eye colour / gender (data whose value is non-numeric)

D data, accurate, precise, repeatable, reproducible

E C

F **one** from: risk of burns – handle with tongs; risk of sparks – wear eye protection; risk of damage to eyes (extreme brightness) – observe burning metal through filter / darkened screen

WS1.3

A results, independent, measurements / readings / observations, mean, units, outliers, repeat, scale, *x*, line graph, bar chart, pie chart

B

Angle (degrees)	Distance 1 (cm)	Distance 2 (cm)	Distance 3 (cm)	Mean distance (cm)

C 80 cm

D $\dfrac{48 + 50 + 55}{3} = 51\,cm$

E *x*-axis – angle of slope (degrees); *y*-axis – mean distance travelled (cm); linear scales, must start at zero for both axes, *x*-axis should not exceed 40°; points plotted at approximately (20, 51), (30, 59) and at (0, 0); (positive correlation)

WS1.4

A data, best fit, curve, conclusion, relationship, scientific, prediction

B as temperature increases, time to dissolve decreases; when temperature doubles, the time to dissolve reduces by less than half

C
  a the point at (6.0, 3.8) should be labelled as an outlier; the best-fit line should only use the other seven points
  b the prediction was correct; more specifically, extension is proportional to force – as force doubles, so does extension; the measurement of extension when force is 6 N is an outlier, far from the trend in the data; it appears to be a mistake; I have not used it to draw the best-fit line

WS1.5

A evaluate, quality, data, improvements, method, confidence, outliers, precise, more, random, systematic, range, more / repeat

B discuss the quality of the data you have collected; suggest and explain improvements to your method so you can collect data of better quality if you do it again

C
  a both groups have similar averages, so have similar accuracy; group 1 has a larger spread of readings than group 2; group 1 might have been less careful, or used a less precise measurement instrument, or it could just be random; group 2 has a larger number of readings than group 1
  b **two** from: take more repeat readings to detect outliers; set up their equipment and take readings more carefully in case they were not using the equipment as well as possible; use a more precise measuring instrument in case that reduces the spread of the results

Working Scientifically Pinchpoint

A this is an incorrect answer – changing variables will **not** improve confidence in the conclusion

B this is an incorrect answer – repetition of readings lets you know the precision of the result; you reduce uncertainty by improving or changing the measuring instrument

C this is the correct answer

D this is an incorrect answer – you need to find ways to **decrease**, not increase, the spread to improve precision

Pinchpoint follow-up

A accurate – close to the true value of what you are measuring; precise – this describes a set of repeat measurements that are close together; repeatable – when you take the measurements of an investigation again and get similar results; reproducible – when other people carry out the same investigation and get similar measurements

B **accuracy**: 1, 3, 4; **precision**: 2, 5

C
  a **two** from: different-sized bubbles, too fast to count, might miss some
  b collect gas in a small measuring cylinder or gas syringe to measure the volume of gas (or other suitable suggestion)

D 2, 4, 5

B1.1

A cells, microscope, magnifies, observation

B slide – **Y**; eyepiece lens – **W**; objective lens – **X**; light – **Z**

C **a** select the objective lens with the lowest magnification; look through the eyepiece and turn the coarse-focus knob slowly until the leaf comes into view; turn the fine-focus knob until the leaf is focused

    b use an objective lens with a higher magnification

    c total magnification = eye piece lens magnification × objective lens
= 10 × 50 = ×500 magnification

B1.2

A nucleus, cytoplasm, cell membrane, mitochondria, cell wall, chloroplasts, vacuole

B animal – clockwise from top-left: cell membrane, cytoplasm, mitochondrion, nucleus; plant – clockwise from top-left: chloroplast, vacuole, cytoplasm, mitochondrion, cell wall, cell membrane, nucleus

C nucleus – contains genetic material and controls the cell; mitochondria – where respiration occurs; cell membrane – barrier that controls what comes into and out of a cell; cytoplasm – where chemical reactions take place

D **a** where photosynthesis occurs

    b contains cell sap to keep the cell firm

    c strengthens the cell and provide support

E cellulose

B1.3

A specialised, red blood, impulses, sperm, hair, water, chloroplasts

B **a** egg cell   **b** nerve cell   **c** leaf / palisade cell

C **a** true   **b** false – they have **no** nucleus (to maximise their ability to carry oxygen)

    c true   **d** false – they contain **haemoglobin or** they **do not** contain chlorophyll

D **a** to allow the sperm to 'swim' towards the egg

    b to transfer energy for movement

    c to enable the cell to move through fluid more easily

E root hair cell – large surface area for absorbing water and nutrients

B1.4

A high, low, diffusion, oxygen, carbon dioxide

B oxygen, glucose

C **B** should show partial mixing of the two types of particles; **C** should show both types of particles evenly distributed

D water diffuses into plant through root hair cells; it moves from the soil where it is in a high concentration to the cell where it is in a low concentration

E water will diffuse into the plant cells and fill up the vacuole; this pushes outwards on the cell wall and makes the cell rigid; this helps the plant to stand upright

B1.5

A euglenas, unicellular, one, cytoplasm, chloroplasts, eye spot, flagellum

B step 1 – nucleus divides; step 2 – cytoplasm divides

C **a** enables it to move / swim (towards light / food)

    b make food by photosynthesis

    c detects light (then euglena moves towards it)

D euglenas are only made of one cell; plants are multicellular organisms

E engulf / surround tiny particles of food (algae / bacteria / plant cells) forming a food vacuole; the food vacuole then digests the food

B1 Chapter 1 Pinchpoint

A this is the correct answer

B this is an incorrect answer – plants **do not** suck up water, it moves into the plant by diffusion

C this is an incorrect answer – particles move from an area of **high** concentration to an area of **low** concentration

D this is an incorrect answer – water (and other) molecules can move into **and** out of cells by diffusion

Pinchpoint follow-up

A the larger the surface area, the quicker the diffusion of useful substances (such as oxygen / glucose) into the cell, or waste products (such as CO_2) out of the cell

B water molecules **diffuse** from one region to another **because** they move from an area of high **concentration** to one of lower **concentration**; this means water moves from the soil to the cell, and then between the cells

C **a** kitchen box circled in first two lines; no box circled in third row   **b** high, low, same

D **a** arrow coming from vacuole pointing to outside of the cell

    b water moves out of the cell as water is in a higher concentration inside the cell so diffuses to a lower concentration in salt water

B2.1

A multicellular, hierarchy, tissues, organ, organ system, organism

B **a** group of similar cells working together

    b group of different tissues working together

    c group of different organs working together

C red blood cell – cell; blood – tissue; heart – organ; circulatory system – organ system; dog – organism

D muscle tissue – contracts to pump blood around the body **or** nervous tissue – stimulates heart to beat

E **a** organ system

    b generation of new organisms (reproduction) / to produce seeds (by production of pollen and eggs / ovules)

B2.2

A respiratory, lungs, oxygen, exhale, trachea, bronchi / bronchus, alveoli / alveolus, gas exchange

B 1 trachea; 2 lungs; 3 rib; 4 diaphragm; 5 bronchus; 6 bronchiole; 7 alveoli

C they maximise diffusion of gases between the lungs and the blood by having: a large number – to create a large surface area; thin walls – only one cell thick; a rich blood supply – to transport gases to / away from the lungs

D **a** higher percentage in exhaled air as it is a waste product of respiration

b lower percentage in exhaled air as some is used in respiration

c percentages are the same, as the gas is not used or produced by the body

B2.3

A ribs, contract, increases, decreases, relax, decreases, increases, out, bell jar, asthma, volume

B muscles between ribs contract, pulling the ribcage up and out; the diaphragm contracts and moves down; the volume inside the chest increases; so the pressure decreases; this draws air into the lungs

C **a** push the rubber sheet up to represent the diaphragm relaxing; the volume inside the chest decreases so the air pressure increases; air is forced out of the balloons (which represent the lungs) so they deflate

b the ribcage / bell jar wall doesn't move, which would further decrease the volume of chest cavity

D (fill a plastic bottle with water and place a plastic tube in the neck of bottle; turn the bottle of water upside down in a tank of water); read the level of water in the bottle; take a deep breath, then breathe out for as long as possible into the tube; read the new level of water in the bottle; calculate the difference in the water levels – this is your lung volume

B2.4

A skeleton, protect, support, move, blood, marrow

B 1 skull; 2 jaw bone; 3 collar bone; 4 vertebral column; 5 radius; 6 femur; 7 kneecap

C muscles are attached to bones; when a muscle contracts it pulls on the bone, causing it to move; joints are where two or more bones join together, and allow bones to move in different directions / independently of other parts of the skeleton

D support – bones create a framework for muscles and organs to connect; protection – stop vital organs from being damaged; making blood – tissue in centre of some bones makes blood cells

E **one** from: skull – brain; vertebral column – spinal cord; ribcage – heart / lung

B2.5

A joints, movement, directions, ligaments, cartilage, contracts, force, newtons

B **a** shoulder is a ball-and-socket joint, which allows movement in all directions; knee joint is a hinge which allows movement backwards and forwards

b the joints are fixed so no movement can occur

C push down as hard as possible onto a newton scale; the reading on the newton scale will be the force exerted by the triceps muscle

D **a** clockwise from bottom-left: ligaments, fluid, cartilage, tendon

b tendon – connects muscle to bone; ligament – connects two bones together; cartilage – smooth tissue that protects the ends of the bone; fluid – makes joint slippery, allowing bones to move without rubbing

c bone marrow

B2.6

A tendons, shortens, bone, muscles, joint, antagonistic, relaxes

B **a** to pump blood around the body

b to squeeze food along the digestive system

c to cause movement

C pairs of muscles that work together to cause movement at a joint; when one muscle contracts, the other relaxes

D **a** muscle B contracts and muscle A relaxes

b muscle C contracts and muscle D relaxes

E when a muscle can no longer contract with the same force (occurs after repeated muscle use)

B1 Chapter 2 Pinchpoint

A this is an incorrect answer – gas exchange occurs quicker when there is a **larger** surface area

B this is the correct answer

C this is an incorrect answer – shape B has a **larger** surface area

D this is an incorrect answer – gas exchange will happen more quickly in shape B as it has the larger surface area

Pinchpoint follow-up

A

Faces	Shape A	Shape B
Top and bottom	2 × 4 = 8	2 × 8 = 16
Front and back	2 × 4 = 8	2 × 4 = 8
Left and right	2 × 4 = 8	2 × 2 = 4
Total	24	28

B villi **increase** the surface area; this **increases** the rate at which nutrients can diffuse from intestine into blood

C **a** $(2 \times (2 \times 8)) = 32$; $(2 \times (2 \times 4)) = 16$;
$(2 \times (4 \times 8)) = 64$
$= 32 + 16 + 64 = 112 \text{ mm}^2$

b bigger than

D evaporate, smaller than, B

B3.1

A adolescence, physical, puberty, sex hormones, taller, pubic / underarm, break / deepen, shoulders, periods, hips

B adolescence is the period of time when a child develops into an adult – it involves both physical and emotional changes; puberty refers only to the physical changes

C **boys** – voice deepens, hair grows on face and chest, shoulders widen, testes start to produce sperm; **girls** – breasts develop, periods start, hips widen, ovaries start to release egg cells; **both** – pubic / underarm hair grows, growth spurt, body odour

D **a** to make space for a baby to grow in the uterus

b to be able to produce milk for a baby if she becomes pregnant

B3.2

A sperm, vagina, testes, sperm ducts, penis, egg, oviducts, uterus

B 1 cervix; 2 ovary; 3 oviduct; 4 uterus; 5 vagina

C 1 testis; 2 sperm duct; 3 glands; 4 urethra; 5 penis; 6 scrotum

D **a** releases an egg cell each month / produces female sex hormones

b ring of muscle which keeps baby in place until it is ready to be born

c receives sperm during sexual intercourse / passage through which baby is born

E sperm cells are made in the **testes** and released into the **sperm duct**; here they mix with fluid from the **glands** that provides nutrients to keep them alive; the mixture of sperm and fluid is called **semen**; semen is released through the **urethra** in the **penis** during ejaculation / sexual intercourse

B3.3

A gametes, sperm, egg, ovary, cilia, ejaculation, nucleus / nuclei, fertilisation, embryo, uterus, implantation

B (egg and sperm meet; the sperm burrows its head into the egg); the nucleus of the sperm cell and the nucleus of the egg cell join together

C male – sperm, testes, sperm duct, flagellum / tail to 'swim' female – egg, ovary, oviduct, pushed / wafted along by the cilia of the cells that line the oviduct

D (sperm released from penis) → vagina → cervix → uterus → oviduct

E divides several times to form a ball of cells / embryo; the embryo attaches to lining of uterus – implantation; here it continues to grow and develop into a baby

B3.4

A uterus, gestation, 9, sac, oxygen, blood, placenta, umbilical cord, cervix, uterus, vagina

B a fetus develops from a fertilised egg, ready to be born

C 1 placenta; 2 umbilical cord; 3 uterus; 4 fetus; 5 fluid sac; 6 cervix

D **a** organ where substances pass between the mother's blood and the fetus's blood such as oxygen and carbon dioxide. It also acts as a barrier to prevent infections and harmful substances reaching the fetus

b fluid acts as a shock absorber, protecting the fetus from any bumps

E mother's cervix relaxes, which causes it to open; uterus walls contract, pushing the baby through the cervix, through the vagina, and out of the body

B3.5

A menstrual, egg, ovulation, lining, period

B day 1 – period / blood from the uterus lining starts to be lost; day 5 – period / bleeding stops and uterus lining begins to regrow; day 14 – ovulation / egg is released from an ovary

C **a** lining of the uterus breaks down and the cycle starts again

b fertilised egg attaches to uterus lining and the woman becomes pregnant, so no period occurs; the uterus lining remains thick

D condom – barrier method – prevents sperm being released into vagina; contraceptive pill – contain hormones which stop ovulation / affect uterus lining; (or other appropriate examples with explanations)

B3.6

A pollen, anther, insects, brightly, nectar, sweet, large, light / low mass, stigma

B 1 filament; 2 anther; 3 petal; 4 stigma; 5 style; 6 ovary; 7 sepal

C transfer of pollen from the anther to the stigma (by wind or insects)

D **three** from: brightly coloured petals – to attract insects; nectar – sweet sugary fluid which bees can use to make honey; produce sticky / spiky pollen – stick to insects; anther / stigma found within flower – so insects can brush against them

E wind – pollen has low mass so can be blown easily by wind; lots produced to increase chance of it reaching another plant; insect – larger mass, less produced; sticky / spiky exterior to stick to insects

B3.7

A fertilisation, pollen, ovule, fruit, seeds, germinate, warmth

B 1 ovule; 2 ovule nucleus; 3 pollen grain; 4 pollen nucleus

C the pollen grain grows a pollen tube down the style until it reaches an ovule inside the ovary; the nucleus of the pollen grain then travels down the tube and joins with the ovule nucleus (fertilisation); the ovary then develops into the fruit and the ovules become seeds

D 1. seed swells and hard **seed coat** splits; 2. first **root** appears (and grows downwards); 3. first **shoot** appears (and grows upwards towards the **light**); 4. plant starts to make its own food by photosynthesis

E $\frac{18}{25} \times 100 = 72\%$

B3.8

A dispersed, competition, space, wind, animals

B **a** wind – seed is light, and extensions act as parachutes / wings (keeping seed in air for longer so disperses further)

   b explosive – fruits burst open when they are ripe, throwing seeds in different directions

C so they are spread far away from the parent plant and other seeds to minimise competition for space / nutrients / water / sunlight

D **a** the larger the wing of the seed, the further it will travel

   b **i** length of seed wing, in cm

      ii distance the seed travels, in cm or m

      iii height seed is dropped from, in cm or m; height of fan, in cm or m; windspeed, in m/s; fan setting

B1 Chapter 3 Pinchpoint

A this is the correct answer

B this is an incorrect answer – the statement should refer to fertilisation occurring in plants **as well as** animals

C this is an incorrect answer – this is the definition of **pollination**

D this is an incorrect answer – this answer is vague and lacks detail. The definition should refer to the **nuclei** of cells fusing together.

Pinchpoint follow-up

A wind-pollinated plant: anthers hang out of flower so pollen is blown in the wind; stigmas also hang out of the flower to catch pollen; covered in 'feathers' to help catch pollen; pollen grain grows tube down style to ovary; pollen nucleus travels down tube to ovary where it fuses with an ovule nucleus – fertilisation; fertilised ovule develops into seed

B animal – sperm, egg, sperm and egg nuclei fuse, fallopian tube, offspring / baby
   plant – pollen, ovule, pollen and ovule nuclei fuse, ovary, seed

C 5, 4, 6, 1, 3, 2

D 1 – pollen tube grows from the pollen grain through the style; 2 – pollen nucleus travels down pollen tube; 3 – pollen nucleus fuses with ovule nucleus – fertilisation

B1 Revision questions

1 **a** **X** petal [1]; **Y** stigma [1]; **Z** filament [1]

   b **i** reproductive / sex cell [1]

      ii anther [1]   **iii** ovary [1]

   c insect-pollinated, e.g. tulip / daisy / sunflower [1]; wind-pollinated, e.g. grass / corn / wheat [1]

   d the nuclei of the pollen and ovule / male and female plant gametes [1] join together / fuse [1]

2 **a** nucleus – controls the activities of the cell [1]; vacuole – stores sap and helps to keep the cell firm [1]; cytoplasm – where the cell's chemical reactions take place [1]

   b [contain chlorophyll] to enable the plant to photosynthesise [1]

3 **a** **six** from: take thin slice of onion material [1]; place on slide [1]; add cover slip [1]; add stain to help view some structures [1]; move microscope stage to its lowest position [1]; place the slide on the stage [1]; select (the objective lens with) the lowest magnification [1]; look through the eyepiece [1]; adjust the coarse focus knob until the cells come into view [1]; then adjust the fine focus knob until the cells are in focus [1]; increase the magnification (use an objective lens with a higher magnification) to view structures more clearly / in more detail [1]

   b sketch shows: a number of cells in a regular pattern [1]; a minimum of three correctly labelled components [3]

   c **i** cellulose [1]

      ii (the cellulose is strong, so the) cell wall is rigid [1] to provide support for the cell / plant [1]

4 **a** alveoli / alveolus [1]

   b transfers gas between lungs and blood [1]; CO_2 out **and** O_2 in [1]

   c large surface area [1] and thin wall / wall only one cell thick [1] to maximise rate of diffusion [1]

5 **a** volume = difference between water levels / 4.0 – 0.5 [1] = 3.5 litres [1]

   b **two** from: exhaled air has: lower proportion of oxygen [1]; higher proportion of carbon dioxide [1]; higher proportion of water vapour [1]; is warmer [1] (or converse)

   c e.g., asthma / smoking [1]

6 **a** mean = $\frac{450 + 410 + 370}{3}$ [1]
      = 410 [1] N [1]

   b e.g., muscle fatigue [1]

c **three** from: the two muscles are antagonistic [1]; as the biceps contracts, the triceps relaxes [1], moving the lower arm upwards [1]; as the triceps muscle contracts, the biceps muscle relaxes [1], moving the lower arm upwards [1]

7 **a** A [1] and C [1]

b $\frac{8}{20} \times 100$ [1] = 40% [1]

c **two** from: an animal will be attracted to eat the plant [1]; the sticky coating on the seeds will stick to the animal's body / fur [1]; the seeds will then be deposited in another area [1]

8 **four** from: cartilage is a smooth tissue [1]; cartilage covers the end of the bone [1]; bones now rub together [1]; results in pain [1]; reduction in movement [1]

9 **a** days 14 → 16 [1]

b egg is released / ovulation occurs around day 14 [1]; egg only lives / remains in body for a few days [1]

c **six** from: sperm are released from testes (into sperm duct) [1]; semen / sperm releases from penis **into** vagina [1]; sperm swim through cervix / uterus [1]; egg released from ovary [1]; sperm meet egg in the oviduct [1]; sperm burrows into egg [1]; sperm and egg nuclei fuse to form fertilised egg [1]; egg divides a number of times to form an embryo (which implants in uterus wall) [1]

d **one** (method and explanation) from: condom (barrier method) [1] – latex rubber prevents sperm being released into vagina [1]; diaphragm (barrier method) [1] – prevents sperm reaching the cervix [1]; contraceptive pill / IUD [1] – contain hormones which stop ovulation / affect uterus lining [1] (or any other appropriate example and explanation)

10 **a** X – anther [1]; Y – stigma / style [1]

b wind pollinated [1]; **three** from: anthers / stamen hang out of the flower – pollen released into wind [1]; stigmas hang out of the flower – to catch pollen blown in wind [1]; lots of pollen released – increase chance of successful pollination [1]; low mass / light pollen – easily carried by wind [1]

11 **a** to keep *Daphnia* alive / so *Daphnia* could get oxygen / respire [1]

b **i** 10 × 4 = ×40 [1]

ii **two** from: unicellular organisms consist of only one cell [1]; organs such as eye can be seen / many different cells present within body [1]; structure size too large (at ×40 magnification) for unicellular organism [1]

c **i** use higher magnification / more powerful microscope lens [1]

ii muscle cell [1] contracts to pump blood [1] **or** nerve cell [1] to stimulate contraction **or** red blood cell [1] to carry oxygen [1]

iii **three** from: nucleus – to control processes which occur in cell / store genetic material [1]; cell membrane – barrier that controls what comes in and out of the cell [1]; mitochondria – where respiration occurs to transfer energy [1]; cytoplasm – where chemical reactions occur to sustain life [1]

C1.1

A particles, different, looks, behaves, arranged, move

B a gold particle is the same size as a silver particle, and the particles in gold and silver are arranged in the same way; but a gold particle has a greater mass than a silver particle, so a 1 cm³ cube of gold has a greater mass than a 1 cm³ cube of silver

C **a** a 1 cm³ cube of hafnium has the greater mass

b a hafnium particle is the same size as a zirconium particle, and the particles in zirconium and hafnium are arranged in the same way; but a hafnium particle has a greater mass than a zirconium particle, so a 1 cm³ cube of hafnium has a greater mass than a 1 cm³ cube of zirconium

D **a** the student can pour the spheres out of each beaker

b the spheres that represent gold have a greater mass than the spheres that represent silver

c the particles are much bigger and heavier in the model than in reality

C1.2

A gas(eous), matter, movement, different

B can be compressed – gas state; can be poured – liquid state and gas state; has a fixed shape – solid state

C **a** its particles are in fixed positions

b the particles touch their neighbours / the particles cannot get closer together

c the particles move throughout the container

D top line – no, no; middle line – yes, no; bottom line – yes, no

E **a** Brooke

b each individual grain of sand is solid, and you cannot pour one grain of sand, so it is solid

C1.3

A melting, faster, away, melting, pure, freezing, slowly

B **a** nine particles, arranged in rows across the bottom of the box

b in the liquid, the particles move in all directions, sliding over each other; in the solid, the particles vibrate on the spot / about fixed points

C

- The particles are moving around more and more slowly
- The particles are arranging themselves in a pattern
- Some of the particles are moving around and some are vibrating about fixed points
- All the particles are vibrating about fixed points
- The solid is cooling down

This is the melting point of the substance

C1.4

A gas, gas, liquid, conserved, boiling

B xenon, mercury, mercury

C bromine at 20 °C – liquid; mercury at 400 °C – gas; xenon at −115 °C – solid

D **a** A, B, C **b** A and C **c** B **d** B

C1.5

A gas, surface, condensation, sublimation

B independent – place (where the Petri dish is); dependent – time for all the water to evaporate; control – amount of water

C **a** 1, 5, 2 **b** 2, 6, 3 **c** 3, 8, 4, 2 **d** 3, 7, 9, 2

C1.6

A mixing, gas, diffusion, stir

B **a** particles spread out throughout the room and randomly arranged

  b the particles move randomly in the air all the time

C **a** dependent; control; independent; control

  b it is difficult to judge exactly when the purple colour has completely spread out

  c the size of crystals can vary considerably, and it is difficult to pick out crystals that are all the same size

  d as temperature increases, the time for the purple colour to spread out will be less

  e the higher the temperature, the faster the particles move

C1.7

A all, collide, force, pressure

B there are fewer particles in jar **Y**, so collisions with the walls of the container are less frequent

C from top – true; not possible to know; true; not possible to know; false; true

C1 Chapter 1 Pinchpoint

A this is an incorrect answer – the particles **do** touch their neighbours in the liquid state

B this is an incorrect answer – oxygen is in the **liquid** state at −200 °C, not in the gas state; the particles are **not** far apart from each other – they are touching their neighbours; the particles do **not** move throughout the container, they move randomly at the bottom of the container

C this is the correct answer

D this is an incorrect answer – oxygen is in the **liquid** state at −200 °C, so its particles are **not** arranged in a pattern – they are arranged randomly; the particles are **not** far apart from each other – they are touching their neighbours; the particles do **not** vibrate on the spot – they move around randomly all over the place, sliding over each other

Pinchpoint follow-up

A **a** **i** the particles are randomly arranged; the particles are at the bottom of the container

    ii the particles are not touching each other

  b diagram showing particles randomly arranged at the bottom of the box; the particles should be touching their neighbours

B from top – gas, liquid, solid, gas, solid, solid

C 58 – random and touching – random, sliding over each other; −5 – random and touching – random, sliding over each other; 60 – random and far apart – random, throughout the container; −10 – regular pattern – vibrating on the spot

D **a** solid – particles arranged in a regular pattern, touching each other; liquid – particles arranged randomly in bottom of box, touching each other; gas – particles arranged randomly, throughout the box, not touching each other

  b in the solid state, the particles vibrate on the spot; in the liquid state, the particles move around randomly, sliding over each other; in the gas state, the particles move around randomly, throughout the container

C2.1

A cannot, Periodic, chemical, symbols

B **a** a substance that cannot be broken down into other substances

  b a one- or two-letter code for an element

C hydrogen – **H**; **helium** – He; zinc – **Zn**; **tungsten** – W; iron – **Fe**; **gold** – Au

D a gold is a good conductor of electricity and not damaged by air or water

b the mass of 1 cm³ of aluminium is much less than the mass of 1 cm³ of gold

c argon does not join to, or damage, other substances

d also poisonous to humans, so might harm apple farmers or eaters

C2.2

A atoms, smallest, atoms, different, many

B e.g. mercury atoms are bigger than copper and zinc atoms; mercury atoms have a mass that is more than three times greater than the masses of copper and zinc atoms; the atom with the greatest radius also has the greatest mass

C a 2, 5

b 1 – an atom is the smallest part of an element that can exist; 3 – the atoms of copper are different from the atoms of zinc; 4 – a single atom of zinc does not have the same properties as a piece of zinc wire

D a as copper melts, its atoms move out of their fixed positions; they no longer vibrate on the spot, but instead move around from place to place, sliding over each other

b one copper atom on its own cannot melt because the properties of copper as a solid and liquid are the properties of many atoms; melting involves a change in the arrangement and movement of its atoms

C2.3

A two, strongly, different, one, molecule

B a **T, V, W, X, Z**

b they include atoms of more than one element; the atoms of the different elements are joined together

C a 2   b 3   c 1   d 2

D a all 3 are solid at room temperature

b **two** from: their melting points are different, the appearance of sulfur is different from the appearance of iron sulfide, iron is attracted to a magnet but iron sulfide is not

c in iron sulfide the atoms are joined together to make one new substance

C2.4

A chemical, number, oxygen, one

B MgO; one atom of calcium for every two atoms of chlorine; nitrogen dioxide; one atom of carbon for every one atom of oxygen, CO; one atom of sulfur for every three atoms of oxygen, SO_3

C 2, 3, 4, 5, 3, 3

D **three** sentences, e.g. ibuprofen is a compound; it is made up of atoms of three elements – carbon, hydrogen, and oxygen; there are a total of $13 + 18 + 2 = 33$ atoms in one of its molecules; there are 9 hydrogen atoms for every one oxygen atom

E a $2 \times 16 = 32$ b $(2 \times 1) + 16 = 18$

c $(13 \times 12) + (18 \times 1) + (2 \times 16) = 206$

C1 Chapter 2 Pinchpoint

A this is an incorrect answer – the **relative numbers of the atoms** of each element must be included in a chemical formula

B this is an incorrect answer – the relative numbers of the atoms of each element should be written to the **right** of each chemical symbol, **not** to the left

C this is the correct answer

D this is an incorrect answer – the chemical symbol for carbon is C, **not** Ca and the chemical symbol for nitrogen is N, **not** Ni

Pinchpoint follow-up

A CO_2, C_3H_8, $C_2H_4O_2$, $C_9H_8O_4$, $C_{14}H_{22}N_2O$

B N_2, H_2O, SO_3, N_2O_4

C from top: C_3H_8, CH_4, CH_3COOH, H_2O, C_2H_5OH

D calcium – Ca, carbon – C, chlorine – Cl, nickel – Ni, nitrogen – N, hydrogen – H, oxygen – O, sodium – Na

C3.1

A new, rearranged, differently, not, energy, catalysts, physical

B a **W** and **Z**

b in **W** and **Z**, the atoms are joined together differently before and after the reaction

C from top: chemical; physical; both; chemical

D a chemical reactions make new substances, but physical changes do not; physical changes are normally easy to reverse, but chemical reactions are difficult to reverse; both physical changes and chemical reactions involve energy changes; in chemical reactions, the atoms are joined together differently after the reaction; in physical changes the atoms are joined together in the same way before and after the reaction

b physical changes are different from chemical reactions because atoms are rearranged and joined together differently in chemical reactions, but not in physical changes

C3.2

A reactants, products, left, right, arrow

B reactants – heptane and oxygen; products – carbon dioxide and water

C a calcium + oxygen → calcium oxide

b sodium + chlorine → sodium chloride

c iron + chlorine → iron chloride

d methane + oxygen → carbon dioxide + water

D a $2Mg + O_2 \rightarrow 2MgO$ **b** $2Na + Br_2 \rightarrow 2NaBr$

c $2Fe + 3Cl_2 \rightarrow 2FeCl_3$

d $C_3H_8 + 5O_2 \rightarrow 3CO_2 + 4H_2O$

E a $2Ca + O_2 \rightarrow 2CaO$ **b** $2Na + Cl_2 \rightarrow 2NaCl$

c $2Fe + 3Cl_2 \rightarrow 2FeCl_3$

d $CH_4 + 2O_2 \rightarrow CO_2 + 2H_2O$

C3.3

A energy, combustion, oxygen, carbon dioxide, water, oxygen

B carbon – carbon dioxide – $C + O_2 \rightarrow CO_2$; hydrogen – water – $2H_2 + O_2 \rightarrow 2H_2O$; heptane – carbon dioxide and water – $C_7H_{16} + 11O_2 \rightarrow 7CO_2 + 8H_2O$

C a volume of water – control; increase in temperature of water – dependent; fuel – independent; distance of flame from test tube – control

b place a shield around the apparatus to reduce the amount of energy transferred to the surroundings instead of to the water

c to make it possible to compare the amount of energy transferred per gram of fuel

C3.4

A one, two, compound, compounds, oxide, carbon dioxide, thermal

B **W** and **Z**

C a lead oxide and carbon dioxide

b strontium oxide, nitrogen dioxide, and oxygen

D potassium carbonate did not decompose under the conditions of the investigation; copper carbonate decomposed most easily; lead carbonate did decompose, but less easily than copper carbonate

C3.5

A physical, products, conservation, reactants

B the same numbers of each type of atom are present before and after the reaction

C a 44 g   **b** 4.4 g   **c** 11.2 g

D a mass does not change   **b** mass increases

c mass decreases   **d** mass does not change

e in **b**, the mass of solid at the start is the mass of magnesium; magnesium joins with oxygen gas from the air (which has mass) to make a solid product, magnesium oxide; this means that the mass of solid product is greater than the mass of solid reactant in **d**, both reactants are in the solid state, and so are both products; this means that the total mass of solid reactants is equal to the total mass of solid products

C3.6

A energy, from, to, increase, from, to, decrease

B the temperatures of both reacting mixtures increase at first, showing that the reactions are exothermic; the temperature change for magnesium is 8 °C, which is greater than the temperature change for zinc (5 °C) so the reaction with magnesium is more exothermic

C a aluminium chloride and magnesium chloride

b aluminium chloride

C1 Chapter 3 Pinchpoint

A this is an incorrect answer – a mass has gas, so when a gas leaves a reacting mixture, the mass of the reacting mixture **decreases**

B this is an incorrect answer – if one of the products of a reactant is in the gas state, the mass of solid reactants is **less** than the mass of solid products

C this is an incorrect answer – in chemical reactions, atoms are rearranged and join together differently; the **total mass does not increase** when new substances are made

D this is the correct answer

Pinchpoint follow-up

A 1, 4

B from top – decreases; decreases, increases

C a In the chemical reaction, the atoms **are** rearranged.

b In the chemical reaction, the atoms are joined together **differently** before and after the reaction.

c There are the **same number** of atoms in the reactants as in the products.

d The total mass of products is **the same as** the total mass of reactants.

D a solid magnesium reacts with oxygen gas from the air, so the mass of solid product is equal to the mass of solid magnesium plus the mass of oxygen that reacts with it

b a gas is produced, so the mass of solid product is equal to the mass of solid lead carbonate minus the mass of carbon dioxide that was produced and escaped to the air

C4.1

A sour, soapy, corrosive, skin, dilute

B from top – wear eye protection; burning your skin

C a the acid in bottle **X** is more corrosive than in **Y**

b there are more acid particles in bottle **X** than **Y**

c add water to bottle **X**

D a the particles produced by both acids and alkalis contain hydrogen atoms

b the particles in alkalis include oxygen atoms but the particles in acids do not; the particles in alkalis have a negative charge but the particles in acids have a positive charge

C4.2

A neutral, red, neutral, alkaline, pH, less / lower, neutral, more / greater

B from top: alkaline, acidic, alkaline

C **a** it is difficult to judge which colour on the pH chart exactly matches the colour observed in the test solution
   b pH probe attached to data logger

D **a** X, W, U, Z, V, Y   **b** V, Y, Z
   c Y – the most concentrated solution of acid is most acidic, so its pH is lowest

C4.3

A neutralised, increases, decreases

B **a** increases
   b so that he can grow crops that thrive at the new pH
   c neutralising acidic lakes

C independent – type of tablet; dependent – volume / amount of acid that the tablet neutralises; control – temperature, concentration of acid, type of acid, mass of tablet

D top right – W, Z; middle – Y; bottom right – V, X

C4.4

A salt, chloride, sulfate, hydrogen

B 4, 6, 2, 1, 5, 7, 3

C **a** magnesium sulfate   **b** zinc chloride
   c copper chloride   **d** sodium sulfate
   e potassium chloride

D **a** magnesium + sulfuric acid →
                      magnesium sulfate + hydrogen
   b zinc + hydrochloric acid → zinc chloride + hydrogen
   c copper oxide + hydrochloric acid →
                      copper chloride + water
   d sodium hydroxide + sulfuric acid →
                      sodium sulfate + water
   e potassium hydroxide + hydrochloric acid →
                      potassium chloride + water

E **a** $Zn + H_2SO_4 \rightarrow ZnSO_4 + H_2$
   b $Mg + 2HCl \rightarrow MgCl_2 + H_2$
   c $CuO + H_2SO_4 \rightarrow CuSO_4 + H_2O$
   d $NaOH + HCl \rightarrow NaCl + H_2O$

C1 Chapter 4 Pinchpoint

A this is an incorrect answer – the pH **increases** after adding sodium hydroxide solution

B this is an incorrect answer – adding water or alkali both make a solution less acidic, so **increasing** its pH

C this is the correct answer

D this is an incorrect answer – adding water makes a solution less acidic, so **increasing** its pH

Pinchpoint follow-up

A **a** Adding water to an acid makes the solution **more** dilute.
   b When an acid is diluted, it has **fewer** acid particles per litre. (or converse answer)
   c The greater the number of acid particles per litre, the **lower** the pH. (or converse answer)
   d Adding alkali to an acid **neutralises** some or all of the acid.
   e Neutralising an acid **increases** the pH of the solution.

B **a** 1   **b** 14   **c** 5   **d** 9   **e** 7

C adding water to an alkaline solution – pH decreases, but not below 7 – the solution has been diluted so there are fewer particles of alkali per litre; adding acid to an alkaline solution – pH decreases, possibly below 7 – some of the alkali has been neutralised so there are fewer particles of alkali per litre; adding water to an acidic solution – pH increases, but not above 7 – the solution has been diluted so there are fewer particles of acid per litre; adding alkali to an acidic solution – pH increases, possibly above 7 – some of the acid has been neutralised so there are fewer particles of acid per litre

D 1, 3, 5

C1 Revision questions

1 **a** a substance made up of atoms of two or more elements, strongly joined together [1]
   b gallium and arsenic [1]
   c gallium + arsenic → gallium arsenide [1]

2 **a** 4 [1]   **b** 8 + 10 + 4 + 2 [1] = 24 [1]   **c** acidic [1]
   d arranged in a regular pattern, touching their neighbours [1] and vibrating on the spot [1]
   e move out of places in their regular pattern to a random arrangement [1]; vibrate faster and faster until all molecules are moving around randomly, sliding over each other [1]

3 **a** a substance that cannot be broken down into other substances **or** a substance that is made of one type of atom [1]   **b** Au [1]
   c in the solid state, particles are arranged in a regular pattern and vibrating on the spot [1]; when a substance sublimes, particles leave their positions in the regular pattern and escape to the surroundings as separate particles, moving around from place to place throughout the container [1]
   d in a physical change, no new substance is made but in a chemical reaction, new substances are made [1]; since no new substance is made, subliming is a physical change [1]

4 **a** one reactant breaks down into two or more simpler compounds or elements [1]

b the gas is both corrosive and toxic [1]; the teacher could not take safety precautions to adequately protect students from the dangers associated with these hazards [1]

c **i** the substances are in the gas state, so their particles are moving around from place to place within the whole container [1]; since the test tube is open, some gas particles escape from it [1]

   ii 2.76 g – 0.60 g [1] = 2.16 g [1]

d 2, 4 [1; both needed for mark]

5 **a** sulfuric acid [1]   **b** neutralisation [1]

c zinc oxide + sulfuric acid → zinc sulfate + water [1]

d $ZnO + H_2SO_4 \rightarrow ZnSO_4 + H_2O$ [2; 1 for correct reactants; 1 for correct products]

e zinc oxide [1]

f heat over a water bath **or** stop heating when about half the water has evaporated and leave in a warm place for a few days [1]

g wear eye protection [1], do not touch hot apparatus [1]

6 **a** base [1]   **b** 11 in bottom row [1]

c $\dfrac{10 + 9 + 10}{3}$ [1] = 9.67 [1]

d the independent variable is categoric [1]

e tablet **X** neutralises the greatest volume of acid [1]

7 **a** Thursday [1]

b an acid [1] to neutralise / remove excess alkali / base [1]

c wear eye protection [1]

8 **a** a material that burns and transfers energy to the surroundings [1]

b exothermic, since energy is transferred to the surroundings [1]

c decrease [1] because the product is formed as a gas, and escapes to the surroundings [1]

9 both evaporation and boiling are changes of state from liquid to gas [1]; boiling involves the formation of bubbles, but evaporation does not [1]; in evaporating, particles leave the liquid surface [1] but in boiling, bubbles of gas also form throughout the liquid, rise to the surface and escape [1]; boiling occurs at the boiling point only [1] but evaporating happens at any temperature [1]

10 **a** liquid, solid, solid [1]

b all three elements are shiny and silver-coloured [1]; mercury is liquid at 20 °C but platinum and silver are in the solid state at 20 °C [1]; mercury and platinum do not react with substances in the air, but silver does [1]

c they are both solid, shiny, and silver-coloured [1]

d platinum does not react with substances in the air, but silver reacts with hydrogen sulfide in polluted air to make an unattractive black substance [1]

e mercury is in the liquid state at 20 °C but platinum is in the solid state (the action of tilting moves a liquid and triggers the alarm, but would not affect a solid) [1]

f the substance is a compound made up of atoms of two elements [1]; there are two atoms of silver for every one atom of sulfur in the compound [1]

g silver sulfide consists of particles of two elements, strongly joined together in a compound, but silver and sulfur each have particles of one element only [1]

h $\text{percentage by mass of sulfur} = \dfrac{\text{mass of sulfur}}{\text{mass of silver sulfide}} \times 100$ [1]

$= \dfrac{216\,\text{g}}{248\,\text{g}} \times 100$ [1] = 87.1% [1]

P1.1

A push, pull (either order), move, direction, shape, gravity, friction / air resistance, air resistance / friction, interaction, measured, newtons / N

B A force of friction of the road on the tyre makes a bus change speed. A force of air resistance of the air on their parachute helps a skydiver land safely. A force of gravity of the Earth on the water makes spilt water spread into a puddle.

C every force is the result of the interaction of two different objects; for air resistance, the object affected must be touching the air molecules; for gravity, the object affected does not need to touch the object causing the gravitational force

D **a**

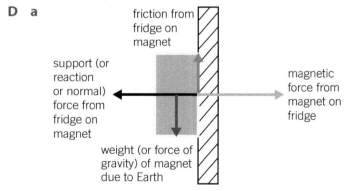

b (weight of magnet due to Earth) weight (or force of gravity) of Earth due to magnet; (friction from fridge on magnet) friction from magnet on fridge; (support force from fridge on magnet) support (or reaction or normal) force from magnet on fridge; (magnetic force from fridge on magnet) magnetic force from magnet on fridge

P1.2

A deform, compress, pushes, reaction, stretch, extension, tension, double, Hooke's Law, proportional, elastic

B $\dfrac{200}{50} = 4$; $1.2 \times 4 = 4.8\,\text{cm}$

C cable – stretch; weight of lift pulls down, support from where it's attached pulls up; tyre – compress; weight of person (bike / wheel rim) pushes down, support force from road pushes up

D the Earth pulls down on you with a force of gravity, your weight; your weight pushes the particles in the floor together; the bonds between the particles in the floor are compressed; the bonds push back and support you

P1.3

A friction, rough, lubrication, air, water (either order), streamlined, slow down

B **a** water resistance causes boat to slow; **b** to reduce friction between metal parts; **c** without friction your shoe would slip uselessly on the pavement, like on ice; **d** air resistance causes the skydiver to fall more slowly

C **a** boat slows down (or speed decreases, or stops); drag (or water resistance) pushes on boat opposite to the direction of its motion; no other force acting horizontally after engine stops, unbalanced force; have to push water molecules (or particles) out of the way to move forward

b box slows down (or speed decreases, or stops); friction pushes on box opposite to direction of its motion; no other force acting horizontally after person stops pushing, unbalanced force; surface of floor is rough when look on small enough scale

D independent – type of surface (cement or ice); dependent – force to move shoe; control (one from) – mass, shoe, angle of surface (horizontal)

P1.4

A fields, non-contact, charge, charge, stronger, gravitational, decreases, gravity, mass

B a force, masses, gets weaker

C Earth's surface – 1600; orbit – 1400; Moon's surface – 260 (to 2 s.f.); far from any star or planet – 0

D nearer to charges in cloud, so stronger field; more likely to be struck by lightning

E the gravitational force is a pull towards the Earth; it is low and keeps decreasing; gravity is a non-contact force – a field – which is why the probe still has this force on it; the field weakens with distance, which is why the force keeps decreasing

P1.5

A balanced, equilibrium, direction, speed, unbalanced, direction, speed (either order)

B **two** from: aeroplane at constant speed (thrust equal and opposite to air resistance); person floating in swimming pool (weight equal and opposite to upthrust); cup on table (support force equal and opposite to weight); any other suitable answer; **not**, e.g., bike speeding up / slowing down / turning corner, Moon orbiting Earth

C **a** any combination showing equal arrows going in opposite direction, such as one each up and down, or left and right

b any combination showing unequal arrows in opposite direction, such as up, down, left but not right; or with at least one arrow not of equal length to the others

c balanced forces are when there are pairs of forces on an object that are equal but in opposite directions so they cancel out, e.g. when the bus is stationary; unbalanced means there is a force that is not cancelled, e.g. when the bus speeds up, the driving force is larger than the resistive forces

D **a** arrow drawn from the centre of the Moon towards Earth, labelled 'force of gravity on Moon due to Earth'

b the Earth pulls the Moon with the force of gravity; it is the only force acting on the Moon, so it is unbalanced and the Moon's velocity causes it to move in a circular orbit

P1 Chapter 1 Pinchpoint

A this is an incorrect answer: there must be an **unbalanced** force to cause a turn but the diagram and statement show balanced forces

B this is the correct answer

C this is an incorrect answer: it correctly states that the forces are unbalanced but the diagram wrongly shows **balanced** forces

D this is an incorrect answer: the diagram is correct but the forces are **not** balanced

Pinchpoint follow-up

A **a** **i** one arrow up from centre of ball labelled 'support force from hand', second arrow same size, down from centre of ball, labelled 'force of gravity from Earth' (or just 'weight')

ii yes **iii** no (it remains stationary)

b **i** a single arrow down from centre of ball, labelled 'force of gravity from Earth' (or just 'weight')

ii no **iii** yes (it is speeding up, towards ground)

B **a** arrow drawn from centre of cyclist pointing to right (towards centre of the circle)

b arrow drawn from centre of cyclist pointing down (towards centre of the circle)

C **a** cyclist pushing road to the left

b arrow from box where their hands touch it, to the right, equal in size to the left arrow

c the person

D **a** balanced, not **b** unbalanced, change, speed up
    c unbalanced, change, turn right **d** balanced, not

P2.1

A wave, energy, amplitude, frequency, wavelength, peak, trough, transverse, longitudinal, close together, further apart, reflection, incident, reflected

B **a** clockwise from bottom-left: trough, amplitude, peak / crest, wavelength **b** transverse

C similarity: **one** from: vibration / oscillation, energy moves / travels in direction of wave, has wavelength / amplitude / frequency; difference: transverse – vibration at right angle to direction of wave, longitudinal – vibration parallel to direction of wave

D **a** most of the wave (energy) is reflected, little energy is absorbed, little energy is transmitted
    b **one** from: if two peaks arrive at the same time, the resulting water wave is higher / double amplitude above central position as the peaks add up; if two troughs arrive at the same time they add up to give lower / double amplitude below central position; if a peak and a trough arrive at the same time, the waves cancel so for a moment the water is not raised or lowered.

P2.2

A vibrate, particles / molecules, vacuum, solid, quickly, light, medium

B sound waves travel faster in solids than gases; particles in a solid are very close together, so the vibration is passed along more quickly than in a gas

C travelling faster than the speed of sound

D light travels much faster than sound, so light takes much less time to travel the same distance; the observer sees the explosion almost immediately, but hears it after a delay

E sound is the transfer of energy through vibrations of particles; space is a vacuum, where there are no particles, so sound cannot travel through it

P2.3

A amplitude, frequency, hertz, 20, infrasound, ultrasound, audible, higher

B lots of animals can hear frequencies that are much higher or much lower than the frequencies humans can hear

C **a** larger amplitude, for example:

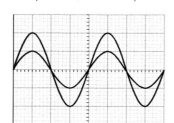

b longer wavelength, for example:

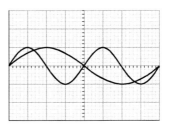

D human – hear a sound – within hearing range; bat – hear nothing – below hearing range; dog – hear a sound – within hearing range

P2.4

A ear, pinna, auditory, eardrum, ossicles, amplify, cochlea, hair, nerve, brain, decibels, damage, diaphragm, electrical, amplifier

B **a** ossicles vibrate and amplify sound
    b auditory nerve transmits signal to brain

C **a** pinna directs sound wave towards auditory canal
    b eardrum vibrates, transmits sound wave to ossicles
    c liquid in cochlea vibrates and causes hairs to vibrate

D loud noises damage sensitive cells at base of hairs in the cochlea; damage can be temporary or permanent; risk of permanent damage increases the louder the noise becomes (wear ear plugs or other hearing protection, stand further away from source of noise, or similar) and the longer you are exposed (use equipment for shortest time possible to get work done, or similar)

E similarity: e.g. something vibrates (ear drum, diaphragm); produces an electrical signal; signal transmitted elsewhere (auditory nerve, wire) difference: e.g. mechanical process in ear (movement of hairs) vs electrical and magnetic process in microphone (movement of magnet near a coil); pinna gathers sound but many microphones have no equivalent

P2.5

A ultrasound, 20 000, sonar, transmitter, reflects / echoes, receiver, time, echo, echoes, reverberation

B **a** sound waves with a frequency too high for people to hear, above 20 000 Hz
    b transmit ultrasound waves; these travel through the woman and reflect off the fetus, producing an echo; receiver detects echo; waves take time to travel; machine measures the time between the transmission and the echo, and calculates the distance using data on how fast the waves travel
    c for example, physiotherapy – ultrasound waves absorbed to treat swelling by heating; depth finding – ultrasound waves echo from seabed, calculate distance from time delay; fish finding – ultrasound waves echo from shoal of fish, calculate distance from time delay

C e.g. sperm whales hunt in deep water, where there is too little light to see by; whale emits sound waves which reflect from its prey and whale detects echo; some dolphins hunt in shallow water where their prey is buried out of sight in the sea bed (similar explanation to whale); some bats hunt at night, when there is very little light to see by (similar explanation to whale)

P1 Chapter 2 Pinchpoint

A this is an incorrect answer – both waves **X** and **Y** have a higher amplitude and are therefore louder, but wave **X** does **not** a higher pitch, it has a lower frequency / longer wavelength (fewer waves per second)

B this is an incorrect answer – wave **X** has a lower frequency / longer wavelength (fewer waves per second), therefore **lower** pitch

C this is the correct answer

D this is an incorrect answer – wave **Z** has a higher frequency / shorter wavelength (more waves per second) and therefore a higher pitch; however, **so does wave Y**. In fact the frequency of **Y** and **Z** is the same; only their amplitude differs.

Pinchpoint follow-up

A **a** R   **b** Q

B more complete waves in same time / shorter wavelength / time interval between neighbouring peaks (or troughs) is smaller / more peaks and troughs, more crossings of the horizontal axis in same time / it goes up and down more often in same time (**not** it goes up and down more, or it goes higher)

C
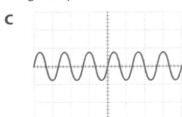

(or similar diagram: higher frequency so more waves, lower amplitude so smaller peak–trough)

D **a** V
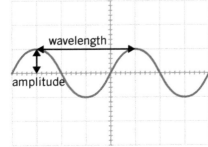

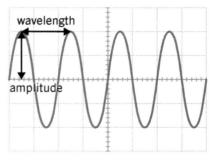

any vertical arrow labelled **amplitude** peak-to-centre, or centre-to-trough; any horizontal arrow same length as shown from peak-to-peak, trough-to-trough, or zero-crossing to similar zero-crossing, labelled **wavelength**

b wave **W**'s wavelength is half wave **V**'s wavelength

P3.1

A luminous, source, non-luminous, reflected, eye, transmit, opaque, translucent, scattered, wave, vacuum, 300 000 000, light-time

B 4, 5, 1, 3, 2 (or 1, 3, 4, 5, 2)

C **a** cat – some reflected and some absorbed
   b glass – transmitted   **c** eye – absorbed

D **a** 300 000 (km/s) × 60 (s/min) × 60 (min/h) × 24 (h/d) × 365 (d/y)
= 9 460 800 000 000 km or 9 500 000 000 000 km (to 2 sig. fig.)
   b 4.2 × 9 460 800 000 000 = 39 735 360 000 000 km or 40 000 000 000 000 km (to 2 sig. fig.)

P3.2

A reflects, reflects, incident, reflected, normal, equal, incidence, reflection, plane, specular, virtual, diffuse

B **a** angle of reflection = angle of incidence (or both angles are the same / equal)
   b diffuse scattering
   c the light rays striking the surface are parallel; however, because the surface is rough, the angle of incidence is different in different places, so the angle of reflection is different

C
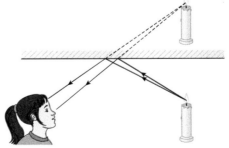

D **a** walls and floor of room are not perfectly smooth; sunlight falls on them and scatters off diffusely, at lots of different angles; some of this enters your eye, making the room appear bright

b things like metal panels on car and shop windows are very smooth; sunlight falls on them and undergoes specular reflection; sometimes when you are in a particular spot you then see the image of the Sun reflected, which is very bright

P3.3

A medium, speed, direction, refraction, slows down, towards, shallower / less deep, converging, focus

B **a** light reflects from the stone and travels up through the water; when it passes into the air it changes speed – slower in the water, faster in the air; this causes the ray of light to bend (away from the normal), called refraction

b

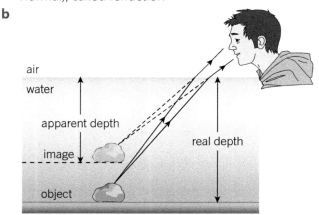

C **a**

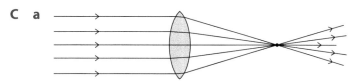

b light refracts as it enters glass from air; it refracts again as it leaves glass; it refracts more further from middle of lens

P3.4

A focusing, object, lens, iris, pupil, retina, photoreceptors, chemical, optic, pixels, pixel, electrical

B object – reflected light from this enters the eye; cornea and lens – focus the light; iris – controls the size of the pupil, allowing in more or less light; pupil – a hole that allows light to enter the lens; retina – where the image forms – contains photoreceptors; photoreceptors – rods and cones – absorb light causing a chemical reaction which produces an electrical signal; image – real (you could put a screen here and you would see an image), inverted, smaller than the object; optic nerve – sends electrical signal to the brain

C light refracts as it passes through the cornea and lens; bends rays to focus them at back of the eye on the retina; pupil allows light to enter; real image; image is inverted; image is smaller than object

D similarities: e.g. image is real, inverted, smaller; focuses light through lenses; light absorbed by detector; both have aperture (pupil in eye); differences: e.g. detector is a charge-coupled device (CCD) or film instead of retina; detection is by a physical reaction instead of a chemical one

P3.5

A primary, secondary, cyan, primary, white, subtract, subtracts, blue, reflecting, blue, prism, spectrum, dispersion, frequency, lowest, continuous

B light refracts as it enters and leaves glass of the prism; white light consists of light of many different wavelengths / frequencies / colours; different wavelengths of light refract by different amounts, this is called dispersion; violet refracts more than red

C primary red added to primary green; our eyes absorb that light, detecting both red and green; we perceive that as the secondary colour yellow

D **a** it will appear black; white reflects all colours, so the red light is reflected to the filter; green filters absorb all colours except green, so no red light is transmitted through the filter, and no light reaches the eye, so the object appears black

b it will appear green; white light consists of all colours, including green; green objects reflect green light and absorb all others, so green light is reflected to the filter; green filters transmit green light, so the green light reaches the eye

E the ball will appear red; secondary yellow light consists of red and green light; the red ball absorbs all colours except red, so it absorbs the green light, leaving the red light to reflect and be detected by the eye

P1 Chapter 3 Pinchpoint

A this is an incorrect answer – the ray must bend **away from** the normal as it leaves the glass

B this is the correct answer

C this is an incorrect answer – it shows the ray being **absorbed** when it reaches the edge of the glass, instead of **refracting** into the air

D this is an incorrect answer – it shows the ray **reflecting** inside the glass, instead of **refracting** into the air

Pinchpoint follow-up

A **a** slower

b light **refracts** (or bends or deflects) **towards** the **normal** when going from a **medium** in which it travels **faster** into one where it is **slower**; it refracts **away** from the normal when passing from **slower** into **faster**

B the bottom of the spoon appears in a different place from the top because light reflected from the spoon through the water refracts as it leaves the water;

bottom of spoon appears larger because curved container means water acts as a lens

C   absorbed, scattered, transmitted, refract, normal, faster, slower, slower, faster

D   mirror, reflected, transmitted, refracts, towards, slows down, away from, speeds up

P4.1

A   satellites, orbit, Moon, natural, planets, Mars, Sun, Solar System, comets, stars, galaxy, Milky Way, Universe

B   a   meteor – rock or dust that burns up as it passes through the Earth's atmosphere
    b   Solar System – the Sun and everything that orbits it
    c   galaxy – a collection of billions of stars
    d   star – a natural, luminous object

C   Proxima Centauri - nearest star (other than the Sun) – 4 light-years; Moon – 1 light-second; Andromeda – nearest large galaxy (other than the Milky Way) – 2 million light-years; Sun – 8 light-minutes

D   **asteroids** are some of the smallest objects in our **Solar System**; they orbit the **Sun**; **Moons** orbit **planets**; many **moons** are larger than most **asteroids**; **planets** are larger than **moons**; they orbit the **Sun**; the **Sun** and everything that orbits it make up the **Solar System**; billions of stars group together to make up our galaxy, the **Milky Way**; billions of galaxies together make up the **Universe**

P4.2

A   Solar, Sun, planets, planets, ellipse, Venus, Mars, rock, gas, gases, moons, asteroid, dwarf

B   asteroid belt – made up of small rocky bodies, between Mars and Jupiter; Sun – in the centre of the Solar System; a planet – orbits Sun, may be rocky or gas giant; a moon – orbits a planet; a comet – made up of ice and dust; sometimes orbits close to the Sun, sometimes far

C   a   all planets nearer the Sun (out to Mars) are rocky and small, lack rings, have few or no moons, and are hotter; all planets further from the Sun (from Jupiter onwards) are large gas giants, have rings, have many moons, and are colder
    b   Neptune is far from the Sun so expect it to be a gas giant, large (50 000 km diameter; if value given, accept 20 000–150 000), cold (–210 °C; accept –270 to –200), with rings, and many moons (14; accept 10–80)

D   similarities: **two** from: orbit Sun; orbits almost circular; some planets are rocky like asteroids
    differences: **two** from: planets are larger than asteroids; most asteroids are found in a belt but planets orbit at very different distances; some planets are mostly made of gas rather than rock like asteroids; planets have atmospheres but asteroids do not

P4.3

A   day / 24 hours, spins, night, year, orbits, tilt, towards, more, longer, higher

B   the Moon – orbits the Earth once a month; the Sun – the Earth spins on its axis once every 24 hours and so different regions of the Earth face the Sun at different times of day; stars – the Earth orbits the Sun once a year and the night-side of the Earth faces different constellations of stars during the year

C   a   Accra will be hottest and Iqaluit coldest, with the others in order of how far north they are; reason: the Sun is nearest to being overhead at Accra so each bit of ground receives more of the Sun's rays; (or converse: Sun lowest over horizon at Iqaluit, etc.)
    b   Accra: 12.4 hours (accept 12.0–14.3); Iqaluit: 20.8 hours (accept 18.0–24.0)

D   there would no difference in day-length and little, if any, difference in temperature between summer and winter; it would still be cooler than at the equator and hotter than the poles

P4.4

A   half, Sun, Earth, phases, new, full, month, Sun, Earth, (either order) umbra, solar, penumbra, solar, Moon, lunar

B   1 – C; 2 – G; 3 – F; 4 – A; 5 – B; 6 – D; 7 – H; 8 – E

C   first quarter; full; third quarter; waning crescent; new

D   a   i   the Moon is between the Sun and the Earth so that it blocks the Sun's light from the Earth
        ii the Earth is between the Sun and the Moon so that it blocks the Sun's light from the Moon
    b   i   new moon, because the Moon is between the Sun and the Earth, and so its dark side must be facing towards the Earth
        ii full moon, because the Moon is on the opposite side of the Earth from the Sun, and so its light side must be facing towards the Earth

E   an eclipse requires a moon, either to block the Sun's light or to go into the planet's shadow; Mercury and Venus have no moon so there are no eclipses visible from there; all other planets have moons and eclipses

P1 Chapter 4 Pinchpoint

A   this is an incorrect answer – **planets** orbit the **Sun**
B   this is the correct answer
C   this is an incorrect answer – solar systems are **smaller** than galaxies
D   this is an incorrect answer – solar systems are **inside** galaxies

Pinchpoint follow-up

A   **three** from: planet, asteroid, comet, meteor
B   option 3 is correct (in option 1 the order of all values has been reversed; in option 2 all values are too small)

C

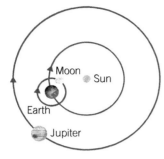

D Proxima Centauri – 4 ✓; Sun – 2 ✓; Jupiter – 3 ✓; Moon – 1 ✓; Andromeda galaxy – 5 ✗

P1 Revision questions

1 **a** gravity [1]
   b **either**: drag (air resistance) from air on parachute [1] and drag from parachute on air [1]; **or** weight (force of gravity) of skydiver due to Earth [1] and weight of Earth due to skydiver [1]; reason: same type of force [1], same pair of objects [1]

2 **two** from: speed [1]; direction [1]; shape [1]

3 particles (molecules) in a liquid / water are closer together than in a gas / air [1]; vibration passed along more quickly [1]

4 **two** from: sharp object puncturing the eardrum [1]; build-up of ear wax [1]; very loud sounds [1]; head injuries [1]

5 similarities: **two** from: orbit Sun [1], elliptical (or nearly circular) orbits [1], spherical shape [1]
   differences: **two** from: Venus mostly made of rock, Jupiter mostly made of gas [1]; Venus smaller diameter (or converse) [1]; Venus nearer to Sun (or converse) [1]; Jupiter has moons, Venus has none [1]

6 the Earth is spinning on its axis (or rotating, throughout) [1]; the Moon and stars moved (almost) the same amount in Figure 3 (or in one hour) due to rotation of Earth [1]; stars are back to (almost) same position in Figure 4 (or in one day) because the Earth takes one day to spin [1]; the Moon has shifted position compared to the stars in Figure 4 (or in one day) because the Moon is orbiting the Earth [1]

7 transverse – oscillation (or motion of source or displacement) is at 90° (or at right angles or perpendicular or normal) to the direction of the wave [1]; longitudinal – oscillation is parallel to direction of wave (or equivalent terms as above) [1]

8 **a** add (or mix) green [1] and blue [1]
   b red – no [1]; green – yes – green [1]; blue – no [1]

9 **a** **two** different transparent media, e.g. light entering glass from air [1]; ray bends towards the normal as it enters denser medium (or converse) [1]
   b light slows down when entering denser medium, e.g. glass (or converse) [1]
   c rays change direction at lens [1]; all rays pass through focus [1]

d as power increases, focal length decreases [1]; focal length changes a lot for small powers (or converse) [1]; the point at 7 cm does not fit trend – it is an outlier / anomaly [1]

10 gravity's effect is strongest while on Earth's surface [1]; gets weaker the further away the probe gets [1]; weight of probe changes but mass stays the same [1]

11 car exerts a force on the bridge (weight) [1]; bridge exerts a force on the car (support) [1]; Earth exerts a force on the car (gravity) [1]; car exerts a force on Earth (pulls the Earth up) [1]

12 **a** $\dfrac{1.2}{1500}$ = 0.000 80 [1] mm [1]; **or** 0.000 000 80 [1] m [1]
   b all 9 points plotted correctly [2; 1 if only 7 points plotted correctly]; correct best-fit line for plotted points [1]
   c directly proportional **or** as force increases so does extension [1]

13 magnetic force and weight are both non-contact forces [1]; fields get stronger when you are closer to the source of the field [1]; that's why the magnet must be close to the iron to give enough force [1]; the Earth's gravitational field is strong and reaches a long way, so the bird is affected [1]

14 **six** from: imaging unborn babies [1]; wave travels through woman and reflects from fetus [1]; receiver detects echo and measures time taken for wave to travel there and back [1]; knowing speed of ultrasound waves, calculate distance to build up image [1] | detecting cancer [1]; (explanation similar to imaging unborn babies) | sonar for depth sounding [1] | sonar for detecting shoals of fish [1] (explanations similar to imaging unborn babies) | shattering kidney stones [1]; wave travels to stone [1]; absorbed and shatters stone [1]; small pieces able to pass out in urine whereas large stone was stuck [1] | ultrasonic cleaning [1]; place jewellery in water bath and pass ultrasound through [1]; dirt particles are vibrated off the jewellery and float off into water [1] | dog whistle [1]; frequency higher than humans can hear but dogs can [1]

15 two waves with same wavelength (number of waves / distance between peaks / troughs) [1] but one with higher amplitude [1]; wave with higher amplitude labelled 'louder' [1]

16 300 000 000 × 60 × 60 × 24 × 365 [1] = 9 460 000 000 000 000 (or 9.46 × 10^{15}) [1] m (to 3 s.f.)

17 **four** from: glass – refract [1], transmit [1], some light reflected [1]; ball – most colours of light absorbed [1], some light reflected [1], blue light reflected [1]

18 **a** quarter: 7 [1]   **b** full: 15 or 16 [1]

19 exoplanet A: mass – accept range 0.1–10 [1]; type – rocky [1]; exoplanet B: mass – accept range 30–3000 [1]; type – gas giant [1]

Periodic table

key

| relative atomic mass |
| **atomic symbol** |
| name |
| atomic (proton) number |

		1
		H
		hydrogen
		1

1	2											3	4	5	6	7	0
																	4 **He** helium 2
7 **Li** lithium 3	9 **Be** beryllium 4											11 **B** boron 5	12 **C** carbon 6	14 **N** nitrogen 7	16 **O** oxygen 8	19 **F** fluorine 9	20 **Ne** neon 10
23 **Na** sodium 11	24 **Mg** magnesium 12											27 **Al** aluminium 13	28 **Si** silicon 14	31 **P** phosphorus 15	32 **S** sulfur 16	35.5 **Cl** chlorine 17	40 **Ar** argon 18
39 **K** potassium 19	40 **Ca** calcium 20	45 **Sc** scandium 21	48 **Ti** titanium 22	51 **V** vanadium 23	52 **Cr** chromium 24	55 **Mn** manganese 25	56 **Fe** iron 26	59 **Co** cobalt 27	59 **Ni** nickel 28	63.5 **Cu** copper 29	65 **Zn** zinc 30	70 **Ga** gallium 31	73 **Ge** germanium 32	75 **As** arsenic 33	79 **Se** selenium 34	80 **Br** bromine 35	84 **Kr** krypton 36
85 **Rb** rubidium 37	88 **Sr** strontium 38	89 **Y** yttrium 39	91 **Zr** zirconium 40	93 **Nb** niobium 41	96 **Mo** molybdenum 42	[98] **Tc** technetium 43	101 **Ru** ruthenium 44	103 **Rh** rhodium 45	106 **Pd** palladium 46	108 **Ag** silver 47	112 **Cd** cadmium 48	115 **In** indium 49	119 **Sn** tin 50	122 **Sb** antimony 51	128 **Te** tellurium 52	127 **I** iodine 53	131 **Xe** xenon 54
133 **Cs** caesium 55	137 **Ba** barium 56	139 **La*** lanthanum 57	178 **Hf** hafnium 72	181 **Ta** tantalum 73	184 **W** tungsten 74	186 **Re** rhenium 75	190 **Os** osmium 76	192 **Ir** iridium 77	195 **Pt** platinum 78	197 **Au** gold 79	201 **Hg** mercury 80	204 **Tl** thallium 81	207 **Pb** lead 82	209 **Bi** bismuth 83	[209] **Po** polonium 84	[210] **At** astatine 85	[222] **Rn** radon 86
[223] **Fr** francium 87	[226] **Ra** radium 88	[227] **Ac*** actinium 89	[261] **Rf** rutherfordium 104	[262] **Db** dubnium 105	[266] **Sg** seaborgium 106	[264] **Bh** bohrium 107	[277] **Hs** hassium 108	[268] **Mt** meitnerium 109	[271] **Ds** darmstadtium 110	[272] **Rg** roentgenium 111	[285] **Cn** copernicium 112	[286] **Nh** nihonium 113	[289] **Fl** flerovium 114	[289] **Mc** moscovium 115	[293] **Lv** livermorium 116	[294] **Ts** tennessine 117	[294] **Og** oganesson 118

*The lanthanides (atomic numbers 58–71) and the actinides (atomic numbers 90–103) have been omitted.

Great Clarendon Street, Oxford, OX2 6DP, United Kingdom

Oxford University Press is a department of the University of Oxford.
It furthers the University's objective of excellence in research, scholarship,
and education by publishing worldwide. Oxford is a registered trade mark
of Oxford University Press in the UK and in
certain other countries

British Library Cataloguing in Publication Data
Data available

978-1-38-203010-6

10 9 8 7 6 5

Paper used in the production of this book is a natural, recyclable product
made from wood grown in sustainable forests.
The manufacturing process conforms to the environmental regulations of the
country of origin.

Printed by CPI Group (UK) Ltd, Croydon CR0 4YY

Acknowledgements

The publisher and the authors would like to thank the following for
permission to use their photographs:

Cover image: Sebastian Tomus/Shutterstock; **p22**: Steve Gschmeissner/
Science Photo Library; **p95**: Kukhmar/Shutterstock.

All artwork by Aptara Inc., Q2A Media Services Ltd., and Phoenix Photosetting